WATERGATE GAMES

WATERGATE GAMES

STRATEGIES, CHOICES, OUTCOMES

DOUGLAS MUZZIO

NEW YORK UNIVERSITY PRESS
NEW YORK *AND* LONDON • 1982

Library of Congress Cataloging in Publication Data

Muzzio, Douglas, 1947-
  Watergate games.

  Bibliography: p.
  Includes index.
  1. Watergate Affair, 1972-   2. Game theory.
E860.M89   364.1'32'0973   81-16964
ISBN 0-8147-5384-1   AACR2

Manufactured in the United States of America

TO BARBARA, JESSICA AND DANIEL

Acknowledgments

This book would not exist were it not for the interest and patience of two people. Professor Steven Brams suggested the original idea, provided invaluable direction, and was extremely generous with his time. I am deeply grateful. Barbara Muzzio, to borrow from Richard Nixon, was a saint. That she put up with me is nothing short of a miracle. For four years, she listened, explored, commented, argued, edited, typed and retyped—longer than any Watergate conspirator, except for Gordon Liddy, spent in jail. Hers might have been a more painful experience.

I would like to thank the following authors, periodicals and publishers for their kind permission to reprint copyrighted materials:

Selections from *Stonewall* by Richard Ben-Veniste and George Frampton, Jr. Copyright © 1977 by Richard Ben-Veniste and George Frampton, Jr. Reprinted by permission of Simon and Schuster, a Division of Gulf and Western Corporation.

Selections from *Blind Ambition* by John Dean. Copyright © 1976 by John Dean. Reprinted by permission of Simon and Schuster, a Division of Gulf and Western Corporation.

Selections from *Not Above the Law* by James Doyle. Copyright © 1977 by James Doyle. Reprinted by permission of James Doyle and William Morrow and Company, Inc.

Selections from *The Friends of Richard Nixon* by George V. Higgins. Copyright © 1974, 1975 by George V. Higgins. Reprinted by permission of Little, Brown and Company.

Selections from *Nightmare* by J. Anthony Lukas. Copyright © 1973, 1974, 1976 by J. Anthony Lukas. Reprinted by permission of Viking Penguin Inc.

Reprinted from *To Set the Record Straight* by John J. Sirica by permission of the publisher W. W. Norton and Company, Inc. Copyright © 1979 by John J. Sirica.

Selections from *The Brethren* by Bob Woodward and Scott Armstrong. Copyright © 1979 by Bob Woodward and Scott Armstrong. Reprinted by permission of Simon and Schuster, a Division of Gulf and Western Corporation.

Selections from *The Final Days* by Bob Woodward and Carl Bernstein. Copyright © Bob Woodward and Carl Bernstein. Reprinted by permission of Simon and Schuster, a Division of Gulf and Western Corporation.

Excerpts from "Unanimity in the Supreme Court: A Game-Theoretic Explanation of the Decision in the White House Tapes Case," *Public Choice*, 32 (Winter 1977) by Steven Brams and Douglas Muzzio. Copyright © 1977 by Center for Study of Public Choice. Reprinted by permission of Center for Study of Public Choice. This article is an early version of Chapter 3, "The White House Tapes Game."

Excerpts from "Game Theory and the White House Tapes Case," *Trial*, 13 (May 1977) by Steven Brams and Douglas Muzzio. Copyright © 1977 by the Association of Trial Lawyers of America. Reprinted by permission of the Association of Trial Lawyers of America. This article is an early version of Chapter 3, "The White House Tapes Game."

Contents

List of Figures

Strategy, I told myself; we needed a strategy.

John Dean, *Blind Ambition*

The next stage [in the evolution of a theory] develops when the theory is applied to somewhat more complicated situations in which it may lead to a certain extent beyond the obvious and familiar.

John von Neumann and Oskar Morgenstern,
Theory of Games and Economic Behavior

Introduction

On June 17, 1972, five men were arrested at the national head-quarters of the Democratic party in the Watergate complex in Washington, D.C. On November 7, 1972, Richard Nixon was reelected president in a landslide, receiving 60.8 percent of the popular vote and 97 percent of the electoral vote. On August 9, 1974, Richard Nixon resigned as president in disgrace, his impeachment in the House of Representatives a certainty, and able to count on only 12 to 18 votes in a Senate trial.

Why Watergate? Why did Richard Nixon fall? Nearly eight years after Nixon's resignation, these questions remain, although "Watergate," as event and metaphor, is the subject of thousands of newspaper and magazine pieces, hundreds of scholarly articles, and scores of books, including the memoirs and reminiscences of almost all of the major Watergate participants. However, much of this work is descriptive and narrative, eschewing explicit and systematic theorizing.

Explanations of Watergate vary widely. Some interpretations accent societal and systemic factors. Others stress institutional impacts. Still others emphasize the psychology of Richard Nixon and the attitudes of his aides and associates.[1] "Why Watergate?" has been answered in terms of Nixon's drive toward an "imperial presidency";[2] the corrupt nature of the American national character and political culture;[3] the decline of American political parties;[4] a split in the American ruling elite;[5] the product of the Vietnam war;[6] and activities by Nixon campaign committee and White House "crazies."[7] The question of Nixon's fall is said to be a result of his "need to fail";[8] his "self hate";[9] his "stupidity";[10] his "madness";[11] and his inability to manage.[12]

The number of such explanations is large.[13] Some contradict others; all are incomplete. What is absent in the Watergate literature are attempts at explanation as Abraham Kaplan defines the term. "An explanation shows that on the basis of what we know, the something to be explained could not be otherwise." There is no theory which provides the "elements of necessity" that "serve as an explanation" of Watergate.[14] It is my intention to begin bridging this "explanation gap" by applying game theory to Watergate events.

Game theory—a theory of rational decision-making—appears to be a particularly useful framework within which to explain the decisions by Richard Nixon, his associates, the special prosecutors, the courts, and members of Congress. A game is a situation in which two or more decision-makers (called "players") have two or more alternatives to choose from (called "strategies"), and for each player the result he will experience (called an "outcome") depends on the choices of all the players and, sometimes, the intrusion of "chance." Players are assumed to act rationally; that is, they make choices that lead to better, rather than worse, outcomes. (A more precise definition of rationality, in the context of games, will be given later).

Game theory's focus on individual choice is crucial. Above all, Watergate involved decisions consciously made in various states of knowledge and ignorance. Obviously, systemic, societal, and psychological factors are important but only insofar as they affect the choices made by Watergate "players." Game theory can uniquely integrate these factors and produce a distillation based on interacting choices. For example, Special Prosecutor Archibald Cox's firing in October 1973, and the subsequent "firestorm," were the result of myriad factors. However, an understanding of the choices of a few men, and the outcomes of these choices, lies at the core of any explanation of the Saturday Night Massacre.

Game theory can explain a wide variety of empirical facts in terms of a few theoretical assumptions (including assumptions about the aims of the players, about the resources and information available to them, and so forth). As with mathematical models generally, game theory generates consequences that are logically unassailable if the reasoning underlying the deductions is correct. Game theory is "amenable to a depth of analysis that would be extremely difficult, if not impossible, for the essayist."[15]

The theory offers a point of view that requires a careful unraveling of a tangle of character motivations and their effects. Among other things, it permits the analyst to discriminate between motivational assumptions that work or do not work (that is, explain or fail to explain behavior). For example, were Archibald Cox and Elliot Richardson men of unalloyed political principle or cold calculating strategists, or both? Was Richard Nixon crazy or a man making rational decisions in situations of risk and uncertainty? What considerations moved the Supreme Court justices in reaching their historic ruling in the White House tapes case (*U.S. v. Nixon*), and did their decision reflect rational choices on their part?

Despite the great promise of game theory as a tool for political analysis, and the veritable explosion of the game-theoretic literature since the publication of von Neumann and Morgenstern's *Theory of Games and Economic Behavior*,[16] much of this literature is bereft of real-world applications, except as illustrative examples. (Game theory has been influential in the development of strategic military thinking; indeed, it lies at the heart of modern deterrence theory.) There have been some article-length applications of game theory to historical and recent political events,[17] but to date there is only one systematic book-length application to a highly complex political situation.[18] As John McDonald has noted, "Real life games are a largely unexplored field, and the art of modeling them is virtually unknown."[19]

This dearth of empirical applications has several causes. Game theorists, for the most part, have been interested in the development of the formal theory; analysts with more substantive concerns have been generally unfamiliar with the theory and its developments. Game theory has also been seen by many as inadequate for the analysis of complex historical situations. According to Karl Deutsch and Leroy Riesebach,

> Game situations . . . can be represented, at least in principle, by means of mathematical models. In practice, variables used in such models often seem to be too few to be realistic, too many to be easily managed, too vague or subtle to be measured, and too controversial to be estimated. . . .[20]

Elsewhere, Deutsch has noted that game thoery is static and, hence, not satisfactory for explanations of dynamic historical situations.[21]

In my opinion, the following analysis demonstrates the incorrectness of Deutsch's criticisms and shows the worth of game theory as a tool for penetrating the complex decision-making situations found in Watergate. I do not attempt a general explanation of Watergate. Rather, I reconstruct particular "games" and explain why the players chose the strategies that they did, based on their preferences, and why certain outcomes resulted from these choices. Since preferences are used to explain choices, and preferences may not be entirely clear, I shall consider alternative orderings and determine what consequences they have. By this means, alternative explanations of Watergate choices will be suggested.

In each game, I shall summarize the historical situation and then model it, that is, construct a simplified representation of the strategic situation that captures its essential features. Specifically, in each game the basis for the decision each player made is reconstructed. His values and goals, the strategies available to him, the outcomes that result from his and other players' choices, and the payoffs or the value players attach to the possible outcomes will be analyzed. The effects of various environmental factors such as the amount of information available to each player, the opportunities to communicate, and so on, also will be examined.

Rational strategies will be analyzed and compared to the actual choices the participants made to ascertain the correspondence of predictions that can be made using game theory and the events that did, in fact, transpire. Alternative strategies, choices open to the players but not taken, will also be examined, for in order to explain a game fully one needs to know what did not happen. "Actions conceived by the players, or seen to be available to them, but not taken . . . have a causal bearing on the actions taken which we know as actual external events."[22]

Obviously, difficulties face the modeler of real-life games. The practical problem of setting forth a real-life game, as John McDonald has noted, lies in the fact that much of the play of the game is "submerged" because the game is played "largely in the mind. Only a small part of the game appears in overt action." Thus, both the players and the analyst have a similar problem: "limited visibility."[23]

The paucity of fully developed applications of game theory to significant historical events results, in part, from the theory's rigid data requirements. The detailed knowledge (or, at a minimum, enough information to make informed inferences) of the goals, the strategies, and the perception and evaluation of outcomes by the participants is often either nonexistent or unavailable. The events related to Watergate, by contrast, are described not only in a large secondary literature but also in primary material from congressional and court testimony and affidavits and interviews with, and articles and books by, Watergate participants themselves. However, this literature is problematic since these works offer a welter of contradictory assessments of motives, goals, and actions. *What* actually happened—let alone the interpretation of *why* players did what they did—is often disputed by people with reputations to preserve and/or axes to grind.[24] Sometimes the problem of establishing the "facts" alone is severe, as it was in the Saturday Night Massacre where the analyst is faced with the *Rashomon* quality of the particpants' reports.

The three games that are analyzed are:

1. Conspiracy breakdown games
2. Saturday Night Massacre game
3. White House tapes game[25]

These games have been selected on the basis of two criteria:

1. The situations analyzed are critical turning points in the Watergate affair as suggested by the literature.
2. They allow the analyst to bring to bear the greatest mix of game-theoretic approaches.

Regarding the first criterion, the conspiracy breakdown games represent the initial and expanding deterioration of the Watergate conspiracy; it is what J. Anthony Lukas terms the "uncover."[26] The Saturday Night Massacre game augurs President Nixon's resignation or impeachment and conviction as serious possibilities. It is truly the beginning of the end, the tran-

sition from the middle phase—represented by the hearings of
the Senate Select Committee on Presidential Campaign Activities (Ervin Committee)—and the end phase, which is dominated
by the confrontation between Nixon and the Supreme Court
examined in the final game. The White House tapes game sealed
Richard Nixon's fate, making his departure inevitable. The Supreme Court decision of July 24, 1974 shattered the president's
justification for withholding evidence and forced the release of
the famous "smoking gun" tape of June 23, 1972, which led to
Nixon's resignation on August 9, 1974.

With respect to the second criterion—to bring to bear the
greatest mix of game-theoretic approaches—my purpose is to
examine games that have been little discussed in the theoretical
and experimental literature. Much of the work in game theory
has focused on zero-sum games and their solutions (for example,
minimax and maximin). Nonzero-sum games have been given
less attention except for "Chicken" and "Prisoner's Dilemma,"
perhaps the most famous of games. Other games that appear to
hold great promise for the explanation of real-world events have
been given far less attention. Among such games analyzed here
are games vulnerable to deception and single dilemma games.[27]

Concepts from game theory are used throughout, though
not always its formal apparatus, particularly when its detailed
application seems inappropriate. When new technical concepts
are introduced, they are defined in the concrete context of the
situation being modeled.

Finally, it is worth noting that there is an irony in the use
of the game theory to explain Watergate; in one of the more
intriguing Watergate analyses, game theory and its theoretical
cousins are seen as a cause of Watergate. In the *Jaws of Victory*
by the Ripon Society and Clifford Brown, the authors see the
cause of Watergate as the "captivation" of

> . . . defense intellectuals, corporate executives, economists, law-
> yers and the large majority of our professionals by the new doc-
> trines of strategic thinking, which include game theory. . . .[28]

1

There is nothing covered that shall not be revealed; neither hid, that shall not be known.
Matthew 10:26

Everyone is now starting to look after their behind.
John Dean to Richard Nixon
March 21, 1973

The Conspiracy Breakdown Games

1.1 Break-in to the Hunt et al. Indictments

In the early morning hours of June 17, 1972, James McCord, the security chief for President Nixon's reelection committee, and four Cuban residents of Miami, were arrested by Washington, D.C. police while they were bugging the headquarters of the Democratic National Committee in the Watergate complex.[1] The supervisors of the break-in, Howard Hunt, a White House consultant, and G. Gordon Liddy, counsel to the Committee to Re-Elect the President (CREP), fled from a nearby listening post.[2]

Within a few hours of the arrest of the burglars, a conspiracy formed to conceal White House and CREP complicity in the break-in.[3] Also the conspirators sought to prevent the exposure of what John Mitchell later termed the "White House horrors"—the Huston plan,[4] the Fielding break-in,[5] the ITT/Dita Beard affair,[6] the illegal wiretaps on newsmen,[7] the McGovern break-in attempt,[8] and other activities with ominous implications. The revelation of these Watergate and other horrors could have dealt "a death blow" to President Nixon's reelection[9] and put many of the participants in jail. The trail of culpability led to the president himself; his closest aides, H. R. Haldeman, John Ehrlichman, Charles Colson; his counsel, John Dean; his closest friend, John Mitchell, the attorney general and later campaign director; Jeb Magruder, the assistant campaign director; and dozens of White House, administration, and campaign aides.

The goal of the coverup was containment: to create the appearance that involvement in the break-in stopped with Liddy and Hunt. Immediately, documents that might link the president and his associates to the break-in were destroyed. The conspirators realized, however, that the money used to pay for the break-in would be traced by the FBI to the reelection committee and then to the White House. An FBI money trace to the donors presented still other problems: campaign finance violations, unreported contributions, and illegal corporate contributions.

Three days after the break-in the president and his men constructed a "national security" scenario, which aimed at keeping the FBI from tracing the CREP money backwards to its donors by having the CIA narrow the FBI investigation, claiming it would imperil CIA "assets" in Mexico (where the laundering of illegal campaign contributions took place). Vernon Walters, the deputy director of the CIA, initially acceded to White House pressure to halt the FBI's money investigation. Walters later reversed himself, but FBI acting director L. Patrick Gray had delayed the FBI's interviews for nearly two weeks giving CREP and White House officials the time to develop and refine their coverup strategy.

With the collapse of the "national security" scenario, the conspirators shifted to the "wildman" scenario. Unable to conceal the fact that Liddy had been authorized $250,000 (and paid $199,000), Dean, Mitchell, Magruder, and others fabricated the story that the money used to finance the break-in had been paid to infiltrate radical groups that could endanger the "surrogate" speakers, members of Congress and cabinet officers who crossed the country urging the president's reelection. According to this scenario, Liddy and Hunt had then gone off on their own to commit the Watergate burglary. Liddy was publicly being painted by the White House as a "wildman . . . strange enough to have pulled Watergate off on his own."[10] Both Magruder and Howard Porter, the CREP scheduler and director of the "surrogate speakers" program, told this story to the FBI in July.

Magruder was crucial; the discovery of his involvement in the discussions that led to the break-in and in the distribution of money to Liddy would necessarily implicate Mitchell and then possibly the president.[11] In late June, Haldeman and Ehrlichman asked Dean whether Mitchell and Magruder should be removed from the reelection committee. There was no love lost between John Mitchell, and Haldeman and Ehrlichman. According to Dean, after the break-in there was "a war of nerves" between the Mitchell faction and the White House faction. "Neither side wanted to budge. Each side waited for the other to confess and shoulder the cover-up alone.''[12] Dean urged that both should go since both might be indicted. On July 1, Mitchell resigned. Magruder remained since Haldeman and Ehrlichman "feared that if fired he might break and end any chances for a successful cover-up.''[13] According to Magruder, if the White House had placed the responsibility of the break-in on Mitchell and him, "it might have discouraged Hunt and Liddy.''[14] Once either of them decided to talk, all of the Plumbers' exploits would have come to light.

To insure the success of the coverup, it was necessary to monitor and, if possible, to control the investigations by the FBI, the United States Attorney, and the grand jury. Either Dean or his assistant, Fred Fielding, sat in on FBI interviews of reelection committee and White House staff. Dean received confidential FBI reports on the progress of the investigation from Gray (who also destroyed material found in Hunt's White House safe) and got reports of the grand jury proceedings from Henry Petersen, head of the Justice Department's Criminal Division, who was overseeing the United States Attorney's investigation. Dean also developed special arrangements with Assistant United States Attorney Earl Silbert that exempted top White House and campaign officials from testifying before the grand jury.[15] Furthermore, Petersen steered the prosecution along a very narrow path; he told Silbert to "[k]eep your eye on the mark [the burglary] . . . we're not investigating the whole damn political thing.''[16]

Nonetheless, "the whole damn political thing" was threatened with exposure in early August when the prosecutors informed CREP's lawyers that Magruder was officially a target of the investigation and would be called before the grand jury. Dean, Mitchell, Magruder, Haldeman, and Ehrlichman fleshed out the perjurious story that Magruder and Porter had given the FBI in July.

On August 16, Magruder, in his testimony before the grand jury, exaggerated by $230,000 the amount of money spent by CREP on certain legitimate activities. Porter again corroborated the cover story. Their perjury was successful. Haldeman was "very pleased" because the White House strategy to "stop the involvement" at Liddy had succeeded.[17]

This success emboldened President Nixon to state at an August 29 press conference that John Dean had conducted a "complete investigation" and found that "no one in the White House staff, no one in this administration, presently employed, was involved in this very bizarre incident."[18] In truth, there was no "Dean Report." Far from investigating, Dean was masterminding the coverup on instructions from Haldeman and Ehrlichman.

On September 15, the grand jury returned indictments against Liddy, Hunt, and the five burglars charging them with conspiring to break into the Democratic national headquarters, burglary and the possession of eavesdropping devices, brought under District of Columbia law, and conspiracy and interception of telephone and oral communications, under federal law. John Hushen, the Justice Department's director of public information, declared that the department had closed its investigation, that there was "absolutely no evidence to indicate that any others should be charged."[19] The next day Attorney General Kleindeinst stated that the investigation by the FBI and the U.S. Attorney had been "one of the most extensive, objective and thorough" in many years.[20] Assistant Attorney General Petersen denied George McGovern's charge that there had been a whitewash and cited impressive statistics to demonstrate the thoroughness of the investigation.[21]

On the fifteenth, Dean met with the president and Haldeman. The mood was one of optimism, indeed, victory. Dean reported, "three months ago I would have had trouble predicting there would be a day when this would have been forgotten but I think I can say that 54 days from now [the November 7th election] nothing is going to come crashing down to our surprise."[22] The president complimented Dean on his handling of the case: "The way you have handled this . . . has been very skillful putting your finger in the leaks that have sprung up here and there."[23] He continued, "We are all in it together. This is war. We take a few shots and it will be over. We will give them a few shots and it will be over. Don't worry. I wouldn't want to be on the other side right now. Would you?"[24] Dean provided the only sobering remark, "Well as I see it, the only problem

we may have are the human ones . . . people get annoyed—
some fingerpointing—false accusations. . . ."[25]

Dean, in the almost three months between the break-in
and the indictments, had held together a shifting multileveled
conspiracy to obstruct justice. Essentially, the conspiracy was
composed of four levels. The lowest level included the indictees
- Hunt, Liddy, McCord and the Cubans. Then there was a mid-
level coverup group - attorneys and midlevel presidential and
campaign aides including Parkinson, O'Brien, Mardian and
LaRue. Next there was a level including Magruder, Mitchell,
and Dean, who oversaw all. Finally, there was the "core"—
Haldeman, Ehrlichman, and Nixon.

The coverup was a success because Hunt and Liddy (and,
to a lesser extent, McCord) had remained silent. With their continued silence, "Watergate" would likely end with guilty pleas
or convictions at their trial.

1.2. Initial Hunt-McCord Game
One of the most asked (though never satisfactorily answered)
questions of the entire Watergate affair is why the prosecutors
failed to break the case between the arrest of the defendants and
their indictments. In his defense, Earl Silbert says that from the
start he believed other, more important, figures were involved
but that indictments were brought only against the seven defendants because

> We ran up against a stone wall in trying to get the cooperation
> of Gordon Liddy, James McCord and Howard Hunt. We got
> turned down stone-cold. We couldn't get any insiders.[26]

> I couldn't understand it. If they were going to have to plead, and
> they were, there should have been at least one of them who'd
> make a deal before he got indicted.[27]

Prosecutorial strategy in cases involving multiple defendants, especially in conspiracy cases, entails attempts to crack
at least one of the conspirators and then turn him on his fellows.
Conspiracy cases are almost always "made" on the testimony
of insiders.

The maintenance of the conspiracy depends on the convergence of interests of the conspirators. When the interests of some diverge from the interests of the rest, people start going to jail. In simple terms, the prosecutor's job is to hasten and worsen such divisions. . . .[28]

Standard prosecuting procedure calls for private negotiation between the prosecutor and each defense lawyer. Each defendant is presented with two options. He can choose to remain silent and, according to the prosecutor, face certain conviction on all counts, with the prosecutor recommending to the trail judge that "the book be thrown at" the defendant. Otherwise, he can plead guilty to a reduced number of charges in exchange for a recommendation of leniency, on the condition that the defendant will agree to testify fully against his co-conspirators.

Each defendant knows that the others are being offered the same or similar deals; he knows that only "the first to crack gets the deal." The rest, "firmly hooked, may plead a hopeless case if they choose, but get no consideration unless they can make (convict) somebody new."[29] (Multilevel or hierarchical conspiracies like Watergate are usually broken by the prosecutors "dealing up." That is, once the low-level conspirators are safely "in the bag," they are immunized and compelled to testify about the involvement of those higher up.)

Thus, the prosecutor attempts to create a situation not only where one or more of the conspirators places more value on defecting from the conspiracy than on cooperating in its continuance, but where each defendant feels irresistible temptations to defect first. However, as Silbert and his colleagues were to learn, though only much later, they were dealing with far more than a "standard" criminal conspiracy. Within a few days of the break-in, the White House had taken steps to counteract the "tendency of persons possessing important evidence or information to want to get their share of the credit by coming forward . . .,"[30] which the prosecutors attempted to nurture.

In the tradition of clandestine operations, Liddy had been assured before the break-in that if caught, he and the others would be taken care of. On June 19, three days after the arrest of the five burglars, Liddy reminded John Dean that "support" had been promised: "the usual in this line of work. Bail, attorney's fees, families taken care of, and so forth. . . ."[31]

Liddy had assured Hunt and, through Hunt's wife, McCord and the Cubans that "everything would be taken care of 'Company [CIA] style'."[32] (Two things are done by the CIA if an agent is caught by the enemy. His expenses and his family are taken care of, and every effort is made to rescue him.)[33]

In fact, Dean, on orders from Haldeman, Ehrlichman, and Mitchell, asked Walters to provide CIA financial assistance to the burglars. Walters refused. The White House then launched a massive covert operation to accumulate large amounts of cash and distribute it secretly to the burglars, Hunt, and Liddy.

During the summer and fall of 1972, prior to the November election, Hunt received approximately $220,000 for himself and the other defendants. (Although, through his wife, he demanded in the vicinity of $400,000 and $450,000). In August after receiving an $18,000 payment, Hunt in a conversation with Charles Colson's secretary spelled out the quid pro quo of the payments—that although he would probably go to jail, "my lips are sealed."[34]

In addition to hush money, promises of clemency were made to Hunt, Liddy, and McCord. Hunt assured McCord that executive clemency would be granted if he remained silent. According to McCord, Hunt spoke "as though it had already been committed." McCord was told that similar proposals were made to the Cubans and Liddy.[35] Magruder was also promised clemency in August, when it appeared possible that he might be indicted.

The Players and Their Strategies

Each of the seven men directly involved in the break-in, from the time of their arrests, was faced with two choices:

1. Cooperate in the conspiracy of silence.
2. Defect from the conspiracy.

However, in the following analysis, only Hunt and McCord are considered true players. The Cubans are omitted since they knew little or nothing of White House or election

committee involvement in the Watergate break-in and the other
"horrors."[36] Liddy is not included since, throughout the entire
affair, he acted as if he only had one strategy: to cooperate. His
commitment to silence was amply demonstrated two days after
the break-in when he offered to be shot.[37]

Outcomes and Their Rankings by the Players
     The probable outcomes of the four possible strategy
choices of McCord and Hunt are presented in matrix form in
Figure 1.1.
     If Hunt and McCord cooperate and remain silent, the
coverup holds; the involvement of White House and reelection
committee officials in the break-in remains hidden, rendering the
"containment" strategy successful. Likewise, the "White House
horrors" never are discovered. The involvement of Dean, Magruder, Porter, Mitchell, Haldeman, Mardian, Nixon, and others
in a conspiracy to obstruct justice remains unknown. Nixon's
reelection chances are virtually unaffected by "Watergate"; the
defendants continue to receive hush money and expect clemency
and "rehabilitation" should they be convicted. Watergate as a
national issue would recede with the continued silence of the
defendants.
     If McCord defected and testified about all he knew, the
coverup would be breached and the "containment" strategy
would be seriously compromised. McCord knew, through Liddy
and Hunt, that Dean, Magruder, and Mitchell were involved in
discussions of Liddy's plans. He also knew that Magruder had
perjured himself in his grand jury appearance. The first Watergate break-in and the attempted break-in of McGovern's headquarters would have come to light.[38] His revelation of payments
to assure silence and offers of clemency would tie White House
and campaign officials to a criminal conspiracy. Nixon's reelection would be jeopardized. If McCord defected and pleaded
guilty, all White House "commitments" to him would end.
McCord would have received a reduced sentence, or, perhaps,
even immunity from prosecution. Hunt would probably continue
to receive money, for he still would have some bargaining leverage with the prosecutors and the White House.
     Hunt's defection posed greater dangers than McCord's

FIGURE 1.1

OUTCOME MATRIX OF INITIAL HUNT-McCORD GAME

		McCORD	
		COOPERATE	DEFECT
HUNT	COOPERATE	A. Watergate coverup holds; conspiracy to obstruct justice intact; White House horrors unrevealed; Hunt and McCord continue to receive hush money; "agent's ethic" holds; Nixon reelected.	B. Coverup and conspiracy damaged, perhaps destroyed; McCord pleads guilty, receives reduced sentence; Hunt continues to receive payments, clemency doubtful; Nixon reelection in danger.
	DEFECT	C. Watergate coverup and conspiracy damaged, perhaps destroyed; "White House horrors" exposed; Hunt pleads guilty, receives reduced sentence; Nixon reelection in greater danger.	D. Watergate coverup and conspiracy damaged, perhaps destroyed; both defectors' ability to plea bargain reduced since they ensnare each other; Nixon reelection in greatest danger.

to the president and his associates. Hunt knew all that McCord knew and much more, particularly of the "White House horrors." Whereas, much of McCord's information was second-hand, hearsay, Hunt's was firsthand. He could tie more White House and campaign officials more tightly to criminal activity.[39] Moreover, Nixon's reelection would be in greater doubt if Hunt revealed all that he knew. "Commitments" to Hunt probably would end.[40] He would receive a reduced sentence, or, perhaps, even immunity from prosecution. McCord would stop receiving "commitments" and would have little bargaining leverage with the prosecutors if he remained silent or only subsequently decided to defect.

If both Hunt and McCord defected, their revelations, if made public, would have been a devastating blow to the president's reelection. However, if both defected, their individual bargaining leverage with the prosecutors would have been reduced. The prosecutors could point out that the value of the testimony of each was reduced since the other had already provided the same information.

These conflicting considerations are now combined into a ranking of the four outcomes by the two players.

Hunt's most preferred outcome is that both men remain silent (outcome A in Figure 1.1) He knew that the White House would meet virtually any demands he made. Also, silence would conform to his "agent's ethic," a product of more than 20 years in clandestine operations for the CIA. Hunt felt certain that he would be acquitted, or the case would be dropped by the prosecutors. Until late fall, Hunt and his attorney, William Bittman, thought they could destroy the prosecutors' case against Hunt with a motion to suppress the evidence taken illegally (without a warrant) from his safe. They assumed that the prosecutors' case against Hunt was built on two highly incriminating notebooks he had left in his White House safe. But Silbert never saw the notebooks, they were destroyed by Dean.

Even if he were to be convicted, Hunt expected to spend only a short time in jail. Hunt's evaluation of the outcomes is represented by the partial preference scale (A,B-C-D). (The comma indicates preference and the hyphen indicates indifference.) Of the three defection outcomes (outcomes B,C and D),

Hunt clearly preferred that he do the defecting and not be left "holding the bag." Thus, outcomes C and D are preferred to B; hence (C-D,B). Likewise, he would prefer that he alone defect (C) and receive the credit for first coming forward with important information; hence (C,D).

Putting these partial preference scales together, Hunt's presumed ranking of the four outcomes (from best to worst), defined by the two strategies of each player (where subscript, H, represents Hunt and subscript, M, represents McCord) is:

A. Cooperate $_H$/Cooperate$_M$;

C. Defect $_H$/Cooperate$_M$;

D. Defect$_H$/Defect$_M$;

B. Cooperate$_H$/Defect$_M$.

McCord's evaluation of the cooperate/cooperate outcome (A) as the best is essentially the same as Hunt's. McCord felt certain that he would never be tried, and if tried, the White House would not allow him to be convicted. McCord, like the other defendants, felt that since the wiretapping had been approved by then Attorney General Mitchell, and since Mitchell had the power of government, he or someone else would get him off; hence, (A,B-C-D).[41] Of the defection outcomes (outcomes B,C and D), McCord, like Hunt, preferred that he defect (B or

FIGURE 1.2
PAYOFF MATRIX OF
INITIAL HUNT-McCORD GAME

		McCORD	
		COOPERATE	DEFECT
HUNT	COOPERATE	A. (4,4)	B. 1,3
	DEFECT	C. 3,1	D. 2,2

NOTE: 1. The first entry of each ordered pair is the ranking by the row player (Hunt), the second entry is the ranking by the column player (McCord). Henceforth, x, y = row player, column player.

2. The circled outcome is a Pareto optimal equilibrium.

3. Outcome D is a Pareto inferior equilibrium.

D) to Hunt defecting alone (C); hence (A,B-D,C). Likewise, McCord would prefer that he defect alone; hence (B,D).

McCord's presumed ranking of the four outcomes is:

A. Cooperate$_M$/Cooperate$_H$;

B. Defect$_M$/Cooperate$_H$;

D. Defect$_M$/Defect$_H$;

C. Cooperate$_M$/Defect$_H$.

If the best outcome for each player is represented by "4," the next-best outcome by "3," the next-worse by "2," and the worst outcome by "1," the rankings of the four outcomes in the Figure 1.1 outcome matrix are presented in the Figure 1.2 matrix. This matrix is a *payoff matrix* though the "payoffs" are only ordinal ranks and not cardinal utilities. Here the first entry of the ordered pair associated with each outcome gives the payoff to the row player (Hunt), the second entry the payoff to the column player (McCord).[42]

In this game, the cooperate/cooperate outcome (A) is the rational outcome. In game-theoretic terms, outcome A is Pareto optimal; that is, there is no other outcome from which Hunt and McCord can obtain greater payoffs without hurting the other. This outcome is mutually best. Hence, each player should choose the strategy associated with this outcome. Both Hunt and McCord should cooperate. Also, this outcome is in equilibrium; neither Hunt nor McCord has any incentive to shift strategies since any change by either will result in an outcome which is inferior for both.[43]

In fact, both Hunt and McCord did choose to cooperate and remained silent. The White House had succeeded in creating a "no conflict" game between Hunt and McCord, that is, a game that included an outcome that Hunt and McCord (and the White House) jointly preferred. In contrast, the prosecutors had failed to "hasten and worsen" possible divisions among the defendants.

However, Silbert insists that the prosecutors still had a plan. Throughout that fall and winter, the prosecutors were still looking to crack one of the seven defendants. "Our strategy was to indict, convict, and then immunize the conspirators so that

we could reconvene the grand jury and get more information.''
The prosecutors believed that "the closer a man gets to the clang
of the prison gate, the more willing he is to talk.''[44]

1.3 Indictments to Trial and Sentencing

In September, Wright Patman, chairman of the House Banking
and Currency Committee, announced he would hold a committee
meeting on October 3 to seek subpoena power to interview more
than 40 people on the Watergate break-in. Among them were
Alfred Baldwin, John Dean, Fred LaRue, Jeb Magruder, Robert
Mardian, and John Mitchell. Had these people been forced to
testify under oath before the November election, not only could
they have caused great embarrassment to the Nixon campaign,
but it is conceivable that the entire coverup would have been
exposed.[45] The White House brought heavy political pressure
to bear on committee members to deny Patman subpoena power,
which they did.[46]

The White House had avoided another serious threat to
the coverup. The Patman hearings would have been the only
official inquiry that faced Nixon before the election. (It was clear
by this time that there would be no trial of the criminal or civil
cases before the election.)

On November 7, 1972, Richard Nixon was reelected president.[47] While the election had provided the motivation for the
coverup, the fact of Nixon's victory put added strain on the
conspiracy. The defendants, led by Hunt, feared that since the
president was safely back in office, he would be less concerned
about what they might disclose and, therefore, would have less
reason to assist them.

Six days after the election, Hunt telephoned Colson to
complain about the failure of the White House and CREP to
meet the defendants' monetary demands. Hunt threatened
Colson,

> . . . this thing must not break apart for foolish reasons . . . we're
> protecting the guys who were really responsible. But now that's
> . . . a continuing requirement, but at the same time this is a two
> way street . . . surely your cheapest available commodity is
> money.[48]

Less than a week later, Hunt became more explicit. After deploring the "wash hands attitude now that the election has been won," he told Colson that "Mitchell may well have perjured himself," that clemency for "cooperating defendants is a standing offer." Most ominously, Hunt reminded Colson that "the Watergate bugging is only one of a number of highly illegal conspiracies engaged in by one or more of the defendants at the behest of senior White House officials. These as yet undisclosed crimes can be proved."[49] The White House got the message. In the last week of November, Hunt's lawyer received $50,000.

On December 8, Hunt's wife was killed in an air crash. Hunt became "a broken man."[50] According to Hunt, he "could not stand the stress of a four to six week trial" and decided to plead guilty in the hope that "leniency would be accorded me."[51] On January 2, Hunt called CREP lawyer, Paul O'Brien, "quite upset"; he wanted to plead guilty, but he wouldn't if it looked like he would spend the rest of his life in prison.[52] Hunt still felt that the White House could turn off the U.S. Attorney's investigation.

Colson told Ehrlichman that it was "imperative" that Hunt be given some assurance of executive clemency.[53] On January 4, Ehrlichman told Colson that the president had approved the offer.[54] Colson told Hunt's lawyer that if Hunt were to get a long sentence, "Christmas comes around every year." Hunt regarded that as a firm promise of clemency at least by December 1973.[55] McCord had also become increasingly difficult as the January 8 trial approached. As we have seen, McCord had remained silent during the summer and the fall because he thought he had the "fix in."

In late October, the prosecutors, believing that "motives powerful enough to insure silence before indictment might erode between indictment and trial," offered to accept from McCord a guilty plea to one substantive count of the indictment.[56] In return for his testimony as a government witness, a recommendation of leniency would be made to the court.

McCord unequivocally rejected the offer since the prosecutors would not recommend any type of sentence which would allow him to remain at liberty. In November, a second plea offer was made by the prosecutors. This offer was essentially the same as the first, except that McCord would have to plead guilty to three counts instead of one. Why the change in the government's position? The prosecutors apparently believed that a McCord without any hope to avoid prison might be less motivated to remain silent—especially after his former employers had accomplished the reelection of the president—than he had manifested before the election.[57]

The prosecutors were again wrong. McCord, like Hunt, felt that he had hit upon a strategy that would guarantee his release. Convinced that the government had taps on the telephones of several foreign embassies, McCord called the Israeli Embassy in September and the Chilean Embassy in October. He then instructed his lawyer to file a motion in court requiring the government to disclose any and all intercepted communications in which he was involved. His theory was that the government, rather than reveal such activity, would dismiss the case against him.

In December, McCord began to feel that he was being set up to take the blame for the break-in. On December 4, Judge Sirica had stated in open court that the jury in the upcoming January trial would want to know who had hired the men for the Watergate operation and why. Two days later, the *Washington Star* carried an article which appeared to McCord to be a story planted by the White House to answer Sirica's question. The article reported that, "Reliable sources state that McCord recruited the Cubans and that they believed that they were working for the president on an extremely sensitive mission."[58] To McCord,

> . . . [t]his appeared . . . to be laying the groundwork for a false claim at the trial that I was the ringleader of the Watergate plot. This would draw attention away from Hunt and Liddy and . . . away from the White House.[59]

That same day, McCord wrote to Hunt that, "as he [Hunt] also knew, the story was untrue, and either he could correct it or I would do so."[60] Hunt was not about to do any such thing. At that time, he was still determined to fight the case, an effort that would have been seriously compromised by any public discussion of his role in the recruitment of the Cubans for various illegal activities.

Thus, the White House, if it did indeed plant the story, had succeeded in setting McCord against Hunt and the other conspirators—something the U.S. Attorney had been unable to do. The interests of the conspirators had begun to diverge.

McCord let it be known through his attorney that he would not remain silent if this approach were used. The White House dropped that tack and stories were next leaked to the newspapers that the break-in was a CIA operation. According to McCord, during the latter part of December, Hunt's attorney, William Bittman, and his lawyer, Gerald Alch, fleshed out the "CIA defense"—that the Watergate break-in was a CIA operation and McCord had been recalled from retirement specifically for the break-in.

This drove a further wedge between McCord and Hunt and the other conspirators. McCord was truly protective of the agency; he would not "turn on the organization that employed me for nineteen years and wrongly deal such a damaging blow that it would take years for it to recover from it," even if it meant the loss of his freedom.[61]

At the end of December, McCord wrote to an old friend, John Caulfield, who was working for Dean:

> . . . if the Watergate operation is laid at the CIA's feet, where it does not belong, every tree in the forest will fall. It will be a scorched desert. The whole matter is at the precipice now. Just pass the message that if they want it to blow, they are on exactly the right course.[62]

The CIA cover story was immediately dropped.

On January 9, the day before the break-in trial began, Mitchell instructed Dean that McCord should get the same promise of executive clemency that Hunt had. Caulfield told McCord, "Plead guilty. . . .You will get Executive clemency. Your family will be taken care of when you get out, you will be rehabilitated and a job will be found for you. Don't take immunity when called before the grand jury."[63] McCord told Caulfield he was not interested in clemency; he had another plan which would prevent him from going to jail (the embassy wiretap strategy).

On January 14, Caulfield told McCord that the White House was studying the wiretap question. (A lie; Dean thought the idea unworkable.) Even if that did not work, he would receive clemency after 10 or 11 months (presumably the same Christmas pardon promised Hunt).

McCord was indignant. He said that while some of those involved in Watergate were going to be convicted, others, like Mitchell, Dean, and Magruder (who was "perjuring himself"), were being "covered for."[64] McCord was particularly incensed at Magruder. "People who I am sure are involved are sitting outside with their families. I saw a picture in the newspaper of some guy [Magruder] who I am sure was involved, sitting with his family. . . . I can take care of my family. I don't need any jobs. I want my freedom."[65]

By January 25, McCord realized the futility of the embassy wiretap scheme. He requested that bail money be furnished, but Dean saw the bail money as presenting too many problems. McCord then threatened to defect. He had plans for "talking publicly" and he would do so when he was "ready."[66]

The Watergate trial began on January 10, 1973. Silbert, in his opening statement, said the prosecution would prove that the Watergate burglary was part of an "intelligence operation" financed with CREP funds. The evidence, he said, would show that Hunt and Liddy were the principal directors of a wide-ranging political spying effort which originated in December 1971. Silbert indicated that the government had no evidence linking Magruder, Porter, or Sloan, the government's witnesses, to the planning of the Watergate burglary.

On January 11, Hunt offered to plead guilty to three of the six counts of the indictment. Sirica, however, rejected this deal between the prosecutors and Hunt because "[i]f Hunt simply pleaded guilty, took his medicine, and went to jail, the chance that we would ever find out what was going on in the case would be reduced."[67] (Hunt expected to have his sentence reduced from five to two years if he agreed to plead guilty.) In questioning Hunt, Sirica emphasized that the charges could mean more than

30 years in prison and more than $40,000 in fines. Hunt then pleaded guilty to all six counts. As he left the courthouse, Hunt told reporters that as far as he knew, no higher-ups were involved in the affair.

Sirica was openly dissatisfied with the prosecution's conception and handling of the case. His threat of extreme sentences was an attempt to change the defendants' evaluation of the possible outcomes since the prosecutors had obviously failed to do so.

Two days later Seymour Hersh, in a front page *New York Times* story, alleged that the Cubans were being paid to follow Hunt's lead and enter guilty pleas.[68] On January 15 the Cubans indeed entered guilty pleas which were accepted by Judge Sirica only after intense questioning. Each was asked whether he had been coerced or induced by payments of money to plead guilty. Each denied that he had been paid or coerced and swore that he had received only expense money. Sirica was openly skeptical of some of their replies. He also questioned the money story presented by Porter, Magruder, and Sloan. (Sirica's instinct was correct but his choice of perjurer was wrong. He pressed Sloan who was telling the truth, and not Magruder, who was lying).

The five guilty pleas left only McCord and Liddy to face the jury. McCord stuck to the game plan. Magruder and Porter followed the plan, too, telling the same false story they had given the grand jury the summer before. Summing up the government's case at the trial, Silbert called Liddy, "the leader of the conspiracy, the money man, the boss"; higher-ups were not involved because McCord and Liddy "were off on an enterprise of their own."[69] On January 30, Liddy and McCord were found guilty on all counts.

The prosecutors had been right that motives that insured silence before the indictment might erode between indictment and trial. Yet, the White House had again succeeded in shoring up the defendants. The coverup continued to hold; no higher-ups were implicated in the break-in. Judge Sirica, however, was not convinced. On February 2 after setting bond for Liddy and McCord at $100,000 each (which neither could raise), Sirica declared that he was "not satisfied that all the pertinent facts that might be available . . . have been produced before an American jury.''[70]

He set sentencing for March 23. The maximum sentence for Liddy could have been 50 years in prison and $40,000 in fines; McCord faced a possible 60 years in prison and $60,000 in fines. Given Sirica's reputation for imposing heavy sentences (he was known as "Maximum John"), the defendants had reason to be concerned.

Despite Judge Sirica's open skepticism, by the end of January Nixon and his aides could see their way out of Watergate in the not too distant future. Things were looking up: the president had negotiated a peace settlement in Vietnam; a Gallup poll showed that an all-time high 68 percent of the public supported the president.

After the inaugural, the White House went through a purge of sorts; those most tainted by Watergate—Chapin, Strachan, Krogh, and Colson left. Magruder was rewarded for his perjury with a $38,000-a-year job as the director of the Office of Program Development in the Commerce Department. (A higher position would have required Senate confirmation; the White House feared that Magruder's perjured testimony might be revealed at Senate hearings.)

There were dangers, however. On February 7, by a vote of 77-0, the Senate established a Select Committee on Presidential Campaign Activities (the Ervin Committee) to conduct a full-scale investigation of the Watergate break-in and the related sabotage efforts against the Democrats in the 1972 campaign. Three days later, Haldeman, Ehrlichman, and Dean met to develop strategies to counter the committee. It was going to take "an all out effort" to contain the investigation because the committee had a broad mandate and subpoena and immunity powers. Furthermore, only Senator Edward Gurney (R-Florida) could be counted on to support unconditionally the White House.[71]

The "bottom-line" question was whether or not the seven defendants would remain silent through the Senate hearings. The three men agreed that the coverup depended on the defendants' continued silence, but Dean reported that they were making new demands for money to remain silent. (The payments had been continued during the late fall and winter, but at a diminished rate.) Money was becoming scarce (LaRue distributed $92,000 that month); there was a fear that the cash would run out.

Nonetheless, as February ended, Dean was again optimistic that the coverup would hold and the Ervin Committee could be handled. On the morning of February 28, Dean told the president:

> We have come a long road on this already. I had thought it was an impossible task to hold together . . . but we have made it this far and I am convinced we are going to make it the whole road and put this thing in the funny pages of the history books rather than anything serious.[72]

During March, the Watergate coverup all but collapsed. The first blow came immediately and from an unexpected source—the Senate Judiciary Committee's confirmation hearings of L. Patrick Gray to be permanent FBI director. "Without solicitation or undue prodding from the senators," Gray volunteered startling new information about Watergate to the effect that as early as July 1972 he had turned over FBI files to Dean; that he had discussed the progress of the inquiry often with Dean and Ehrlichman; and that he had allowed Dean to sit in on FBI interviews with Watergate figures.[73]

By March 1, Dean, who had never been linked in an incriminating way with Watergate, had become the central figure. Senators Tunney, Byrd, and others were calling for Dean to testify. (On March 13 the committee voted unanimously to "invite" Dean to testify.)

The president and Dean agreed that he could not testify since too much could come out that would damage both men and perhaps blow Watergate wide open. On March 2, Nixon, citing "executive privilege," publicly declared that "no President could ever agree to allow the counsel to the President to . . . testify before a committee."[74]

This approach to the Gray hearings quickly became part of the president's Ervin Committee strategy. A theory of "executive privilege" was publicly set forth on March 12, which the president hoped would allow Dean and other White House aides to avoid direct testimony before any congressional committee.

By mid-March, as his position was becoming exposed, Dean was having doubts about the maintenance of the cover-up and his role in it. On March 13, he warned Nixon, "There are dangers. . . . There is a certain domino situation. If some things start going, a lot of other things are going to start going. . . ."[75] Nixon was more graphic: "Sloan starts pissing on Magruder and then Magruder starts pissing on who, even Haldeman."[76]

Dean was more and more the focus of attention as Gray talked. He noticed how everyone was hiring his own lawyer, how everybody was looking to "cover his own ass."[77] The money demands, particularly Hunt's, were getting out of hand.

Hunt and the other Watergate defendants were set to be sentenced on March 23, "A date whose finality conditioned my [Hunt's] every move and thought."[78] Hunt was angry that he had received no family "support money" since his wife's death on December 8. (Presumably, $60,000 paid in February was for "legal fees.") Facing a prison cell, Hunt says, he desperately needed money. On March 16, he demanded $130,000 and threatened that if he didn't get his money he would "review his options" regarding "a number of seamy things" he had done for Ehrlichman.[79]

With the coverup beginning to unravel, John Dean, on the morning of March 21, attempted to explain to Richard Nixon that the Watergate coverup had become "a cancer . . . close to the Presidency—that's growing."[80] Dean told Nixon that some way had to be found to bring the affair to a close since the coverup was about to collapse under its own weight. Dean warned that the White House was being blackmailed, that even people who had not yet committed perjury would soon have to do so to protect other people:

> It'll cost money. It's dangerous. . . . If this thing ever blows and we're in a cover-up situation, it'd be extremely damaging to you . . . some people are going to have to go to jail. . . . It's something that is not going to go away.[81]

But Nixon was only interested in Hunt's blackmail demand. When Dean told Nixon that it would cost "a million dollars over the next two years," Nixon replied that "you could get a million dollars and you could get it in cash."[82] Time and again, Nixon came back to the money for Hunt: "Don't you have to handle Hunt's financial situation damn soon? . . . You've got to keep the cap on the bottle that much in order to have any options. . . ."[83] Nixon feared that Hunt would crack under Sirica's threat.[84]

Haldeman explains the apparent lack of understanding between Dean and the president by the different goals the two men were seeking. Nixon wanted "to make certain Hunt didn't talk of his activities that touched indirectly on Nixon, ranging from the surveillance of Teddy Kennedy to Ellsberg." Dean wanted immunity for himself. "Dean intended to use the Hunt blackmail demand and . . . other selective tidbits . . . as the 'shocker' that would awaken Nixon to the danger—and lead him to grant Dean, the man who knew most about Watergate, immunity."[85] Later that day, John Ehrlichman joined the conversation.

> He had a goal of his own. . . . Ehrlichman bore the weight of the Ellsberg break-in as an albatross. . . . The last thing he wanted was witnesses like Dean testifying with immunity. If one of them . . . revealed the Ellsberg break-in, Ehrlichman was finished. And with immunity, they might talk.[86]

Instead of immunity, Ehrlichman suggested a report by Dean, which "the President could use as a basis for saying this was as much as he knew about the matter and the White House was not involved."[87] Dean began to feel that he was being set up by Haldeman and Ehrlichman to take the blame for Watergate.[88] As later events confirmed, his concern was well founded.

Dean had concluded earlier that somebody would have to "walk the plank" to end Watergate. Dean came up with Mitchell and Magruder.

> They were the logical candidates. They had authorized the break-in—and that was what everyone wanted to hear about . . . Mitchell . . . the first Attorney General to go to prison. No one would show the slightest interest in a cover-up; no one had.[89]

Nixon, Haldeman, and Ehrlichman had reached the same conclusion.[90]

However, it was too late. Events had overtaken the president's and his aides' efforts to stem Watergate. On Friday,

March 23, Dean's worst fears had come to pass. One of the defendants, McCord, had "blown."

1.4. Final Hunt-McCord Game

At the sentencing of the seven defendants, Judge Sirica read a letter he had received from McCord two days before. McCord wrote that he felt "whipsawed" by conflicting pressures.[91] On one hand, his answers might be used against him in future appearances before the Ervin Committee, in a civil suit or at some future trial. On the other hand, "to fail to answer your questions may appear to be noncooperation and I can therefore expect a much more severe sentence."[92] McCord charged:

> "1. There was political pressure applied to plead guilty and remain silent.
> 2. Perjury occurred during the trial of matters highly material to the very structure, orientation and impact of the government's case and to the motivation of and intent of the defendants.
> 3. Others involved in the Watergate operation were not identified during the trial when they could have been by those testifying.
> 4. The Watergate operation was not a C.I.A. operation. . . ."[93]

After reading McCord's letter, Sirica said he would take the letter "under advisement" and put off McCord's sentencing to a later date.

With this "preliminary matter" out of the way, Sirica began the sentencing of the other six defendants. He lived up to his reputation as "Maximum John." On five of the defendants he imposed the maximum terms under the law: 40 years each to Bernard Barker, Eugenio Martinez, Virgilio Gonzalez and Frank Sturgis; 35 years to Howard Hunt. However, Sirica made their sentences "provisional"; he would review them after three months, after the defendants had the opportunity to cooperate with investigators. Although the crimes they had committed were "sordid, despicable, and thoroughly reprehensible," he said that they might mitigate their sentences if they testified "openly and completely regardless of what the implications are to yourself or anyone else" before the grand jury and the Ervin Committee. Although Sirica did not hold out any "promise or hopes of any kind," he stated that should the defendants decide

to "speak freely" he would "weigh that factor in appraising
what sentence will be finally imposed in each case."[94] To make
certain that the five men clearly understood the consequences
for continued silence, Sirica imposed an extraordinarily severe
sentence on Liddy. He sentenced him to a minimum of six years,
eights months in jail with *no* provision for review and no bail
until Liddy paid a $40,000 fine.

Strategies, Outcomes and Their Rankings

A variety of factors merged to lead to McCord's defection. The catalyst for McCord's action was Sirica's threat of a
severe sentence for "noncooperation." According to Sirica,
McCord defected because

> . . . unlike the other men charged in the break-in case McCord
> was not willing to go to jail to protect those who approved the
> operation. Despite repeated promises from the White House that
> he would serve no more than a year in prison . . ., [h]e was
> devoted to his family and concerned about the effects of the
> situation on them.[95]

McCord, more than any of the other defendants, wanted
to avoid a lengthy sentence. Liddy was a fanatic. Hunt was a
spy and, by the time of his sentencing, a beaten man with little
to live for. The Cubans were only taking orders; they knew little
and may have been more afraid to talk than not to. McCord—
despite his years in the CIA and his loyalty to it—was a tech-
nician, much less the clandestine agent than Liddy and Hunt
were. McCord was deeply involved in his church, his commu-
nity, his family. He had married his college sweetheart and was
the father of three children, one of them a retarded girl for whom
he felt great responsibility.[96]

Judge Sirica's threat of extraordinarily severe sentences
had changed the nature of the outcomes that resulted from the
interaction of Hunt's and McCord's strategies. Before Sirica's
intervention, the cooperate/cooperate outcome (outcome A,
Figure 1.1) meant a "well-paid year of incarceration."[97] Sirica
had redefined the consequence of continued silence to be a virtual life sentence. As a result, McCord changed his evaluation
(preference ranking) of the outcomes.

By the time of his sentencing, McCord clearly most preferred to break his silence, to defect, while Hunt maintained his silence, cooperated, (outcome B in Figure 1.3b); hence, (B,A-C-D). It is also reasonable to assume that after Sirica's intervention, McCord also preferred that both Hunt and he defect (D) to both of them cooperating (A); he preferred any possibility to receive a reduced sentence; hence (D,A). Being "left holding the bag" (C) remains his worst outcome; hence (B,D,A,C). Hunt, on the other hand, continued to rank the outcomes as he had in the past (A,C,D,B).

If the best outcome for each player is represented by "4," the next-best by "3," and so on, the rankings of the four outcomes in both the initial and final Hunt-McCord games are presented in the payoff matrices in Figure 1.3.

In this final game, McCord's "defect" strategy is *dominant*, that is, defecting is better than cooperating for McCord whatever Hunt does. (A payoff of "4" is better than "2" if Hunt cooperates; and "3" is better than "1" if Hunt defects.) Hunt, recognizing McCord's dominant strategy, knew that if he continued to cooperate his worst outcome, (B), would be the result. So, he should also defect, guaranteeing his next-worst outcome, (D). In fact, in early April, after realizing that there was no longer any point in remaining silent, Hunt decided to testify fully.

McCord's defection was truly the beginning of the end of the coverup. Without his defection the case would never have been broken since "until the prosecutors harvested McCord or Hunt, they had no access to the minimum of facts needed to map the territory of the coverup conspiracy."[98]

1.5. Dean-Magruder Game

McCord's letter did not go into detail as to the identity and roles of those who had planned and financed the Watergate burglary. Nonetheless, it sent "shock waves" among the conspirators at the White House; there were a lot of "scared characters around town."[99] John Dean and Jeb Magruder were rightly among the most frightened.

Before McCord's defection and Gray's revelations, Dean,

FIGURE 1.3
a. INITIAL HUNT-McCORD
(CONSPIRACY MAINTENANCE) GAME

McCORD

	COOPERATE	DEFECT
HUNT COOPERATE	A. (4,4)	B. 1,3
DEFECT	C. 3,1	D. 2,2

b. FINAL HUNT-McCORD
(CONSPIRACY BREAKDOWN) GAME

McCORD

	COOPERATE	DEFECT
HUNT COOPERATE	A. 4,2	B. 1,4
DEFECT	C. 3,1	D. (2,3)

Hunt has no dominant strategy, anticipates McCord's choice.

McCord has dominant strategy.

NOTE: 1. x, y = Hunt, McCord.
2. In the first game, McCord's preference ranking is (A,B,D,C); in the second, (B,D,A,C). Hunt's preferences are the same in both games, (A,C,D,B).
3. The circled outcomes are the rational outcomes.

like his fellow higher-level conspirators (except for Magruder), had been very successful in insulating himself from the investigators and circumscribing his involvement in the coverup. Magruder, although at various times a target of the investigation, had escaped indictment and had been bolstered with promises of financial support and clemency. Magruder and Dean had been playing cooperatively (outcome A in Figure 1.4); there was no thought of their going to the prosecutors; hence (A,B-C-D). Dean and Magruder played a game identical to the initial Hunt-McCord game (Figure 1.2). The payoff matrix of this game is presented in Figure 1.4. Since both Dean and Magruder were satisfied with the cooperate/cooperate outcome (they each received their best outcome), they had no incentive to defect.

FIGURE 1.4
PAYOFF MATRIX OF
(PRE-McCORD) DEAN-MAGRUDER GAME

MAGRUDER

		COOPERATE	DEFECT
DEAN	COOPERATE	A. (4,4)	B. 1,3
	DEFECT	C. 3,1	D. 2,2

NOTE: 1. x, y = Dean, Magruder.
2. The circled outcome is the rational outcome; it is Pareto optimal.

The events of late March changed the game being played by Magruder and Dean. Three days after the McCord letter, the *Los Angeles Times* reported that McCord had told Ervin committee investigators that Magruder and Dean had advance knowledge of the Watergate break-in.[100] This and L. Patrick Gray's remark before the Senate Judiciary Committee that Dean "had probably lied" to the FBI had firmly placed Dean in the public spotlight.[101] At the same time, Dean began to feel that the White House was finally acting upon his March 21 advice "to cut the losses"[102] by cutting loose John Dean. The clues were plentiful.

Reacting to the *Times* story, presidential press secretary Ziegler "flatly" denied that Dean had any prior knowledge of the break-in. Ziegler declared that the president had "absolute and total confidence" in Dean and had told Dean that himself.[103] (Ziegler avoided such sweeping denials regarding Magruder's possible involvement, signaling that he was getting cut loose.) In fact, Dean had not spoken to the president; he sensed that he was being "set up."[104] George Higgins graphically constructs the scenario.

> The President and his inner circle knew . . . damned right well that he'd had no knowledge of plans to bug Larry O'Brien. The next public utterance, or the one after that, would reassert that he knew nothing of the cover-up. Then from some mysterious source would float some rumor that Dean had run the cover-up, which in fact he had, and then there would be some startled-fawn official reactions, and perhaps an investigation by Ehrlichman,

and then, by God, a shamefaced admission: old Dean fooled us. String him up, the bastard.[105]

Haldeman's increasing pressure on Dean to write a Watergate "report" fit the scenario. What the president, Haldeman, and Ehrlichman had in mind was a report that implicated Magruder and others at CREP in the bugging. It probably would have condemned Mitchell, while playing down the existence of any coverup and clearing the White House entirely.[106] If the true story later came out, the president could claim he relied on Dean's report.

Haldeman triggered Dean's survival instinct when he told Dean that the president was going to announce that he was requesting Dean to appear before the grand jury without immunity. Dean subtly parried that he would have no problem appearing before the grand jury, but his testimony on the nature of the Liddy meetings would conflict with Magruder's. He described "other problems," including payments to the defendants, the Hunt threat, and Colson's clemency discussions.[107] The president decided to drop his announcement plans.

On March 26, when Dean was told by Haldeman that the White House was cutting Magruder and Mitchell loose, he realized that everybody except the president was expendable, including John Dean.[108] Dean knew that Mitchell would not crack; Magruder was something else. Dean felt that Magruder either would quickly cave in and "reach out to grab everybody he can hang on to" or that he and Mitchell, under White House direction, would turn on him.[109]

On the twenty-sixth, Dean called his lawyer, Thomas Hogan, who suggested they contact Charles Shaffer, a tough former Assistant U.S. Attorney who had prosecuted Jimmy Hoffa. On Friday, March 30, Dean retained Shaffer. That afternoon and throughout the weekend Dean told Hogan and Shaffer what he knew of Watergate. On Monday, April 2, Hogan and Shaffer informed the prosecutors that Dean was ready to cooperate. Dean began gingerly telling his story to the prosecutors on April 8.

Magruder was slower in perceiving his danger. Magruder initially felt that he could survive the McCord revelations because McCord's testimony was uncorroborated, hearsay.[110] He was further bolstered when Haldeman and Mitchell were "extremely reassuring" concerning "financial support and, if necessary, executive clemency."[111]

However, on March 30, Magruder finally realized that the end was near. The *Washington Post* reported that the Ervin Committee had subpoenaed Magruder's former administrative assistant, Robert Reisner. Magruder knew Reisner could firmly tie him to the planning of clandestine activities with Liddy.[112] Magruder met with Mitchell and Dean to get their assurance that they would stick by the story they had all agreed on the summer before—that they had held only one meeting with Liddy merely to discuss the new campaign finance law. Mitchell readily agreed since the story protected him, but Dean refused to give Magruder any such promise.[113]

On March 30, Magruder saw James Bierbower, a prominent Republican lawyer. After a preliminary talk, during which Magruder stuck to his story, Bierbower agreed to represent him. For ten more days, Magruder maintained the lie. James Sharp, a former U.S. Attorney from Maryland, who had recently joined Bierbower's firm, refused to believe Magruder. He urged Magruder to tell what he knew before it was too late to claim some immunity from prosecution. On April 10, Magruder told Sharp the full story of Watergate as he knew it. On April 12, Sharp and Bierbower opened negotiations with the prosecutors. On the thirteenth, they got a deal they could not refuse—a one-count felony indictment punishable with a maximum of five years in prison in exchange for Magruder's cooperation.

Strategies, Outcomes, and Their Rankings

By the beginning of April, Dean and Magruder were faced with two choices:

1. Cooperate to maintain the conspiracy.
2. Defect from the conspiracy.

The probable outcomes of the four possible strategy choices of Magruder and Dean are presented in the matrix in Figure 1.5.

Dean clearly believed that he would be best off if he went to the prosecutors and told them what he knew about the bugging

FIGURE 1.5
OUTCOME MATRIX OF (POST-McCORD) DEAN-MAGRUDER GAME

MAGRUDER

	COOPERATE	DEFECT
COOPERATE	A. Coverup conspiracy holds for time being; eventual collapse likely; Magruder and/or Dean possible White House scapegoats; in event of collapse, prosecutors deal harshly with Dean and Magruder.	B. Coverup conspiracy cracks; Mitchell, Ehrlichman, Dean directly (Haldeman indirectly through Strachan) tied to criminal activity; Magruder gets "first come, first saved" deal from prosecutors.
DEFECT	C. Coverup crumbles; Mitchell, Ehrlichman, Magruder, Haldeman, and Nixon directly tied to criminal activity; Dean gets "first come, first saved" deal from prosecutors.	D. A composite of outcomes B and C, except Magruder's and Dean's bargaining leverage reduced.

DEAN

and a good part of the coverup (outcomes C and D). He believed that Liddy had begun talking to the prosecutors, that he was a "dead duck anyway."[114] He knew that he would be called to testify either before the grand jury or the Ervin committee at almost any time. By defecting, he could ensure that the full story came out (and on *his* terms), that he would not get blamed as the sole architect and engineer of the coverup; hence (C-D,A-B). If he were the first major figure to defect from the conspiracy (C), he could expect to receive consideration for coming forward; hence (C,D,A-B). Dean would prefer at least the possibility of the coverup's holding (A) to its (and his) destruction on Magruder's (or the White House's) terms and to go to jail "a disgraced scoundrel" (B); hence (C,D,A,B).[115]

Magruder, like Dean, came to prefer the defect outcomes (B and D). "The grand jury was reopening its investigation, the Senate investigation was about to start, McCord named me, Reisner would implicate me, Dean might challenge my sworn testimony—all in all, my story hadn't a chance of surviving"; hence (B-D,A-C).[116] Magruder's lawyer had convinced him that it was just a matter of time before the prosecutors knew the whole story and "right now they need us" (B).[117] However, if Dean defected (particularly if he defected first) Magruder's testimony would be far less valuable; hence (B,D,A-C). If Dean cooperated and did not reveal Magruder's perjury, Magruder's story had at least a chance of surviving (A), which was surely preferable to remaining silent while Dean was telling the prosecutors his version of Watergate; hence (B,D,A,C).

If the best outcome for each player is represented by "4," the next-best by "3," and so on, the rankings of the four outcomes in the Figure 1.5 matrix are presented in the payoff matrix in Figure 1.6.

Both Dean and Magruder have a dominant strategy—to defect. Both do, outcome D results, and they each receive their second-best payoff "3."

Dean-Magruder Game as Two "Mirror-Image" Games

Since Dean and Magruder did not make their choices simultaneously or in total ignorance of each other, the repre-

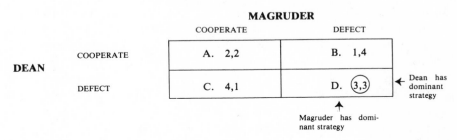

FIGURE 1.6
PAYOFF MATRIX OF
(POST-McCORD) DEAN-MAGRUDER GAME

NOTE: 1. x, y = Dean, Magruder.
        2. The circled outcome is the rational outcome.

sentation of the game in Figure 1.6 does not fully capture the dynamics of the historical situation.

As we know, Dean decided to defect and actually had spoken to the prosecutors before Magruder decided to talk. At the time of Dean's defection, Magruder had not yet changed his original evaluation of the outcomes and he believed that Dean continued to assess the outcomes as he had in the past (that is, Magruder believed that Dean and he were still playing the Figure 1.4 game).

But Dean, by early April, was playing a different game which is represented by the payoff matrix in Figure 1.7. (In this game, the outcomes and Dean's ranking of them are the same as in the Figure 1.6 game, pp. 37–40). In this game, Dean chose his (now) dominant defect strategy, producing the best outcome for him, C, with a payoff of ''4.'' Magruder, thinking that the choice of his cooperate strategy would continue to result in his most preferred outcome, A, with a payoff of ''4,'' was actually at outcome C, giving him his worst payoff ''1.''

This situation did not last. Magruder, after he changed his ranking of the outcomes and still unaware that Dean had already defected, thought he was playing the game represented in Figure 1.8 which is the mirror image of the Figure 1.7 game. (In this game, the outcomes and Magruder's ranking of them are the same as in the Figure 1.6 game, pp. 37–40). Magruder chose

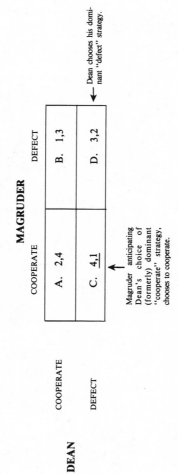

FIGURE 1.7
ACTUAL DEAN-MAGRUDER
GAME AFTER DEAN DEFECTION

MAGRUDER

	COOPERATE	DEFECT
COOPERATE	A. 2,4	B. 1,3
DEFECT	C. 4,1	D. 3,2

DEAN

Magruder anticipating Dean's choice of (formerly) dominant "cooperate" strategy, chooses to cooperate.

← Dean chooses his dominant "defect" strategy.

NOTE: 1. x, y = Dean, Magruder.
  2. Dean's ranking of the outcomes is the same as in "Post-McCord," Figure 1.6 (C,D,A,B). Magruder's is the same as in "Pre-McCord," Figure 1.4, (A,B,D,C).
  3. Underlined outcome is the (temporary) result of the game.

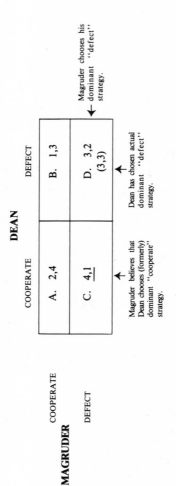

FIGURE 1.8
APPARENT DEAN-MAGRUDER
GAME AFTER MAGRUDER DEFECTION

DEAN

	COOPERATE	DEFECT
MAGRUDER COOPERATE	A. 2,4	B. 1,3
DEFECT	C. 4,1	D. 3,2 (3,3)

Magruder believes that Dean chooses (formerly) dominant "cooperate" strategy.

Dean has chosen actual dominant "defect" strategy.

Magruder chooses his dominant "defect" strategy.

NOTE: 1. x, y = Magruder, Dean.
2. Magruder's ranking of the outcomes is the same as in "Post-McCord," Figure 1.6 (B,D,A,C); Dean's is the same as in "Pre-McCord," Figure 1.4 (A,C,D,B).
3. Underlined outcome is apparent outcome (to Magruder).
4. Payoffs in parentheses are actual payoffs of the defect/defect outcome as represented in Figure 1.6.

his (now) dominant defect strategy. Believing that Dean was continuing to cooperate, Magruder thought *he* had achieved his best outcome, C, with a payoff of "4" (and, as a result, leaving Dean with his worst outcome).

In actuality, Magruder's defection moved the historical game (represented for both players in Figure 1.6) to outcome D where both Dean and Magruder achieved their second-best outcome. It is ironic that both Magruder and Dean, while thinking that they were choosing strategies that gave the other his worst payoff, had both succeeded in producing their second-best.

Dean defected, and the Watergate coverup collapsed, because Dean felt that what George Higgins has termed the "central principles of treachery" were about to be applied to him.

> Paramount among them is the understanding that while the conspirators may hope, desperately, for the permanent success of their undertaking, they may not achieve it. Thus adjustments may be necessary, and when in the course of criminal events, it becomes needful to leave one of the plotters holding the bag, one leaves him, without piercing remorse, holding the bag. The necessity is regrettable, of course, and it would be nice, from the point of view of those still in the clear, if the sacrifice were not demanded, but there it is.[118]

Once the decision to defect was made, speed was of the essence. If Magruder and the others "beat him to the courthouse door," Dean would lose the advantages that go to an "early, 'voluntary' cooperator."[119]

Dean won the race. According to Magruder, "The chronology of the affair proves that [Dean] was about ten days smarter than I was."[120]

1.6 Silbert Ploy

Among the most important factors in John Dean's decision to turn on his fellow conspirators was his belief that Gordon Liddy had begun talking to the prosecutors. This belief was the result of a simple but brilliant ploy, born of desperation, by Assistant United States Attorney Earl Silbert. On March 26, the prosecutors reconvened the Watergate grand jury and in the following days got orders from Judge Sirica granting the seven defendants immunity from further prosecution in return for their testimony before the grand jury. Liddy, intransigent to the end, refused to testify. However, the prosecutors kept the silent Liddy in an anteroom for hours making it appear that he was "spilling his guts." They asked his attorney, Peter Maroulis, to notify the reporters outside that Liddy was, indeed, cooperating. Instead, Maroulis stormed out and strongly protested to the press that Liddy was remaining silent—exactly as the prosecutors hoped he would—persuading many that Liddy was indeed talking. Dean first contacted his attorney, Thomas Hogan, that afternoon.

Even after McCord's revelations, Liddy remained the key to the coverup. McCord's allegations were of tremendous consequence as we have seen. Nonetheless, they were hearsay; all that McCord knew, or Hunt for that matter, of the involvement of Magruder, Dean, and Mitchell in the break-in planning, came from Liddy. Liddy also could expose the Fielding break-in. Of the seven defendants, only Liddy "could bring the whole house down."[121]

The Outcomes and Their Ranking by the Players
With Liddy's continued silence, the Dean-Magruder game had remained at the cooperate/cooperate outcome (outcome A in Figure 1.4). It was a "no-conflict" game; both players received their highest payoff "4". Although the best outcome for the two players, it was clearly the worst for Silbert, who, although not a player, was certainly an interested party who would be affected (receive a "payoff") by the strategy choices of Dean and Magruder.

Silbert naturally preferred to have both Dean and Magruder reveal what they knew (D); next he preferred that one of them do so (B or C). However, since Silbert could not evaluate the impact on his investigation of Dean's versus Magruder's testimony, he is considered to be "indifferent" regarding these outcomes. His preference ranking is (D,B-C,A).

The problem facing Silbert was to structure a "game" such that Dean or Magruder, or both, would come to prefer the outcomes of their defection strategy over the outcomes of their cooperation strategy. The only way he could do this was through deception.

A game-theoretic model of deception has been developed by Steven Brams.[122] Reduced to its simplest terms, the model shows that one player, unsatisfied with the outcome of a game, can deceive another if he can misrepresent his preferences and have this misrepresentation believed. The deceiver can do this because it is assumed he knows the deceived's preference ranking, while the deceived does not know the deceiver's (true) preference ranking. For the deception to be successful, the deceived must not have a dominant strategy and the misrepresentation must make it appear that the deceiver has a dominant strategy. Lacking a dominant strategy, the deceived will choose the strategy that gives him the higher payoff associated with the (apparent) dominant strategy of the deceiver.

Although I assume that Silbert was unaware of the requirements of the formal model, he structured a situation (a game) where the postulated conditions and predicted behavior of the players were successfully met (for him and for Dean and Magruder as well). More specifically, Silbert first had to convince Dean and Magruder that Liddy had become a player in a game involving them (conceptualized below as a two-person game with Dean). Dean had justifiably considered Liddy "the rock of the cover-up."[123] Recall that Liddy was not considered a player in the Hunt-McCord games since he had only one strategy to cooperate, regardless of what anyone else did. However, with McCord's defection, the immunization of the seven defendants, and his extremely severe sentence from Sirica, Liddy very well could have reached his limit and considered defecting (or actually defected). Silbert, then, had to convince Dean and Magruder that Liddy had actually changed his evaluation of the outcomes such that he shifted his strategy choice to defect. Liddy's several hour session with the grand jury, and Maroulis' extreme protestations certainly indicated that Liddy had defected. Dean accepted Silbert's misrepresentation.

Silbert did not know for certain what Dean's preference ordering of the outcomes was. He did know (implicitly) that Dean's defect strategy was not dominant since he would have chosen it. Therefore either Dean had a dominant cooperate strategy or he had rationally chosen to cooperate, given Liddy's dominant strategy to cooperate. If Dean had a dominant cooperate strategy, he could not be deceived (since by definition a dominant strategy provides the best payoff *whatever* the choice of strategy by the other player—whether misrepresented or not). But if Dean did not have a dominant cooperative strategy (which he did not), he could be deceived.

Essentially, Dean believed he was involved in a game with Liddy, while in fact he was playing against Silbert, who was masking as Liddy. Before Silbert employed his deception ploy, the game "played" by Liddy and Dean is represented by the payoff matrix presented in Figure 1.9(a).

In this game, Liddy prefers to cooperate, whatever Dean or Magruder do (outcome A or B); hence (A-B,C-D). Clearly, he preferred that the coverup hold (A); hence (A,B,C-D). Since Liddy apparently never considered defecting, it is impossible to establish a strict ranking of outcomes C and D. Any of three possible rankings—(A,B,C,D). (A,B,D,C), or (A,B,C-D)—produce the same result since Liddy strictly preferred both A and B to both C and D. That is, Liddy's "cooperate" strategy is dominant. Knowing this, Dean, if rational, will choose the strategy associated with his better payoff given Liddy's choice, that is, Dean will also choose to cooperate, receiving his highest payoff "4" (versus "3" if he defected). This outcome is a Pareto-optimal equilibrium; there is no incentive for either Liddy or Dean to shift his choice of strategy. This outcome is clearly the worst for Silbert.

The only way Silbert can induce Dean to choose to defect is to misrepresent Liddy's preferences to make it appear that Liddy ranks the outcomes such that he has a dominant strategy to defect. Since in the historical situation it appeared to Dean that Liddy *had* defected, Silbert's misrepresentation made it appear that Liddy strictly preferred outcomes C and D to outcomes A and B; hence (C-D,A-B). It is also reasonable to assume that Dean believed Liddy would prefer that the conspiracy hold (A) to Dean's defecting unilaterally (B); hence (A,B). Dean clearly preferred that the coverup hold and his involvement in criminal activity remain hidden (A); hence (A,B-C-D). Of the

three defection outcomes (outcomes B,C and D), he surely preferred to defect (B or D) and to defect alone (B); hence (B,D,C).

If Liddy's (false) preferences (C,D,A,B) are combined
with Dean's (true) preferences (A,B,D,C), the payoff matrix of
the game is presented in Figure 1.9(b). If Dean accepted Silbert's
representation that Liddy had decided to defect, he would
choose, if he were rational, that strategy providing him the higher
payoff associated with Liddy's presumed strategy choice. That
is, he would choose to defect since outcome D is preferred to
outcome C.

In the historical game, Dean was not playing against Liddy
but, through Silbert's deception, was playing against Magruder.
Dean defected; Magruder, recognizing this, should also defect,
which he did. Both players received their second best outcome
(outcome D in Figure 1.6).

Silbert was not content just with employing his grand jury
ploy. In his first face-to-face meeting Dean on April 8, just as
Dean was beginning to tell his story "off the record," Silbert
told Dean, "Liddy's been talking to us privately. Now nobody
knows about that but your story is going to square with his."[124]
According to Dean, his reaction was "Jesus Christ. . . . If he
slipped off the mountain it was all over. I started to blurt out
what Liddy knew, but checked myself. I didn't know how far
he had broken."[125] When Dean asked Silbert what Liddy had
revealed, Silbert replied, "you know I can't get into that, John.
His conversations are as privileged as yours."[126] This lie nailed
down Dean's defection. Liddy's presumed defection weighed
heavily on his actions over the next two weeks.

Silbert's grand jury ploy, buttressed by his lie, was not
only crucial in leading Dean to talk but also critically affected
the breadth and depth of his revelations. Remember that "only
the first to crack gets the deal"; the rest, "get no consideration
unless they can make (convict) somebody new." Dean could
and did convict somebody new—as Haldeman, Ehrlichman, and
Nixon were to learn.

To Lie or Not to Lie

Brams' model and its application to the prosecutors' deal-
ings with John Dean clearly illuminate the circumstances under

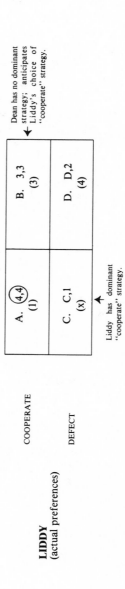

FIGURE 1.9
a. LIDDY-DEAN GAME
BEFORE SILBERT DECEPTION

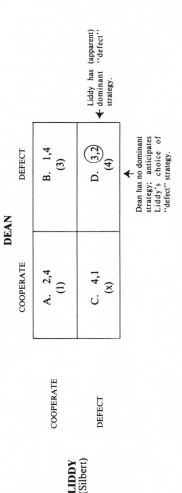

b. APPARENT LIDDY-DEAN
AFTER SILBERT DECEPTION

DEAN

	COOPERATE	DEFECT
COOPERATE	A. 2,4 (1)	B. 1,4 (3)
DEFECT	C. 4,1 (x)	D. (3,2) (4)

LIDDY (Silbert)

Dean has no dominant strategy; anticipates Liddy's choice of "defect" strategy.

Liddy has (apparent) dominant "defect" strategy.

NOTE:
1. x, y = Liddy (Silbert), Dean.
2. Liddy's ranking of outcomes C and D in 1.9a is unknown. Any of three possible rankings (A,C,B,D), (A,B,D,C) or (A,B,C-D) produce the same result given the strict preference of both A and B to C and D respectively, for Liddy.
3. Dean's perception of Liddy's ranking of the 1.9b outcomes is assumed to be (C,D,A,B).
4. Silbert's preferences (in parentheses) are (D,B,A) in both games. Outcome C is not considered since Liddy's defection is not real, hence, (x).
5. The circled outcomes are the rational outcomes.

which some rational actors are motivated to lie and other rational actors induced to accept the lie and act upon it. Silbert, through the use of deception, had restructured the "game" he was playing with Dean so that instead of meeting with failure, he had broken the most serious political scandal in American history.

One of the paradoxical features discovered by Brams in his development of the formal model, and confirmed in the above analysis, is that the deceived is sometimes better off (that is, receives a higher payoff) by being deceived. If Dean had not been so firmly convinced by Silbert's misrepresentation of Liddy's preferences, and had not so quickly acted upon his belief, Magruder might have "beat him to the courthouse door." If that were the case, Dean would have initially received his worst payoff "1" (outcome B, Figure 1.7) instead of his best payoff "4" (outcome C, Figure 1.6). Also, as this example demonstrates, deception, from a normative perspective, is, on occasion, socially desirable.

The "Silbert ploy" was not, as we have seen, the only factor leading to Dean's and, subsequently, Magruder's defection. But clearly this game was a crucial strategic variable in Dean's and Magruder's evaluation of the outcomes of their parallel game represented in Figure 1.6.

1.7 The "Core" is Reduced to One

By the end of the second week in April, the Nixon "team," which had held together so well for months, was falling apart. While Nixon was admonishing his aides, "I don't want people on the staff to divide up and say, 'Well, it's this guy that did it, or this guy that did it,'"[127] Magruder described it as "every man for himself."[128] Nobody trusted anybody; Haldeman, Ehrlichman, Dean were taping their conversations with each other and any potential witness.[129] Lawyers warned their clients not to talk freely with their former colleagues. Dean had spoken to the prosecutors; Magruder was about to. Haldeman and Ehrlichman were developing strategies to serve Mitchell as "the Big Enchilada" to the prosecutors. Mitchell was ignoring any suggestions from his old antagonists that he take responsibility for the break-in. As Haldeman and Ehrlichman plotted about Mitchell,

Dean began to intensify his conversations with the prosecutors about the coverup.

With mounting suspicion, the president and Dean dealt with each other through Haldeman and Ehrlichman. Neither was sure what the other was up to. By early April, Nixon knew that Dean had contacted the prosecutors but he did not know Dean was talking to them directly and what he was saying. However, the president was resisting Haldeman's and Ehrlichman's advice to dismiss him.

The weekend of April 14 and 15 was the most frantic and crucial time for the president and his men since the break-in ten months earlier. Friday evening, April 13, Ehrlichman was told by Colson that Hunt was going to testify fully before the grand jury the following Monday, baring White House and election committee complicity in the Watergate break-in planning and corroborating McCord's allegations of payoffs, clemency offers, and perjury. Haldeman, Ehrlichman, and Nixon agreed with Colson that "once Hunt goes on, that's the ball game."[130] Saturday morning Nixon ordered Ehrlichman to tell Mitchell that afternoon that he should "voluntarily make a statement and admit 'I am morally and legally responsible.'"[131]

Mitchell refused, flatly denying any responsibility for Watergate. Dean was the second candidate for sacrifice. ("Give them an hors d'oeuvre and maybe they won't come back for the main course.")[132] Ehrlichman favored keeping Dean on in the hopes that he would be more favorably treated by the prosecutors as the president's counsel than as a private citizen. Obviously, such favored treatment would have been beneficial to him and Haldeman. Dean was worried that Ehrlichman would try to get Mitchell and Magruder "to turn on me" by agreeing to "some phony story about how *I* gave Liddy the go-ahead."[133]

Magruder called Haldeman on Saturday afternoon and told him what he had told the prosecutors that morning. Magruder warned that "the whole thing is going to blow . . . there isn't anybody that is going to hold."[134]

Dean met with Haldeman and Ehrlichman and presented them with a long list of people he felt had criminal liability stemming from Watergate. The first two names on the "'Post'— break-in" list were Haldeman and Ehrlichman.[135] Late that evening the prosecutors, who had agreed to keep the information

Dean was giving them confidential, called his attorney, Charles Shaffer, and told him they would have to break the agreement. The prosecutors then met with Attorney General Kleindeinst and Assistant Attorney General Petersen and told them what they had learned from Dean and Magruder. The prosecutors had concluded that there was a "putative" case against Mitchell, Mardian, LaRue, Magruder, Dean, Ehrlichman, and Haldeman.

The next day Petersen told the president that Dean was attempting to provide enough evidence to seek immunity from prosecution. Shaffer had warned that unless Dean were given immunity, "We are going to try Ehrlichman, Haldeman, Nixon and this whole administration, that's going to be our strategy."[136]

Petersen reported these threats to the president. He advised Nixon to dismiss Haldeman and Ehrlichman because of their apparent involvement in the coverup but urged that Dean be retained since he was cooperating with the prosecutors in exposing the coverup.

Contrary to Petersen's advice, the president decided that Dean should leave the White House and Haldeman and Ehrlichman should stay. The "core" was all that remained of the Watergate conspiracy. Furthermore, according to Haldeman, after Nixon learned from Petersen that Dean was not holding anything back, the president was "devoted solely to his own survival—and he acted to that end."[137]

Dean met Nixon on Sunday evening to inform him of his discussions with the prosecutors. The president asked whether Dean had received immunity. Nixon instructed him not to discuss national security matters or presidential conversations with the prosecutors. (That afternoon Dean had provided the prosecutors with a copy of the Huston Plan and evidence on the Fielding burglary in an unsuccessful attempt to get immunity.) Nixon then attempted to "clarify" his March 21 comment that it would be no problem to raise one million dollars in hush money for Hunt.

The president was afraid of what Dean might reveal in his efforts to secure immunity; he had to find out what Dean was telling the prosecutors. The next afternoon (April 16) he pressed Petersen on the status of Dean's negotiations with the prosecutors. Petersen told the president that there was no deal but that he was considering granting Dean immunity if he could be used to convict "higher-ups" (the only ones higher than Dean were Mitchell, Haldeman, Ehrlichman, and Nixon himself). Later, Nixon presented Dean with two letters of resignation for him to sign "just for the file."[138] To Dean the letters were confessions of his involvement in Watergate. He recalls, "I visualized Judge Sirica announcing that since Liddy had gotten twenty years, I deserved no less than forty."[139] Dean demurred; instead he presented his own letter which did not mention Watergate and tied his resignation to Haldeman's and Ehrlichman's. The central principles of treachery were going to be applied equally.

On the morning of the seventeenth, Haldeman, Ehrlichman, and Nixon met to develop plans for dealing with Dean. Their discussion ended with the president deciding to tell Petersen that he did not want anybody on the White House staff given immunity. Later in the afternoon, the president began playing "hardball" with Petersen. Nixon warned him that any immunity grant to Dean would be interpreted as a "straight deal" on Petersen's part to conceal the fact that Petersen had provided Dean with grand jury information the previous summer. The president did not care whether Petersen immunized Strachan or other "second people"; he did not want Petersen giving immunity to Dean.[140]

An hour later, the president publicly put forward the "scenario" he, Haldeman, and Ehrlichman had agreed upon:

> On March 21, as a result of serious charges which came to my attention, some of which were publicly reported, I began intensive inquiries into this whole matter.
>
> Last Sunday afternoon, the Attorney General, Assistant Attorney General Petersen, and I met at length in the EOB [Executive Office Building] to review the facts which had come to me in my investigation and also to review the progress of the Department of Justice investigation.
>
> I can report today that there have been major developments in the case concerning which it would be improper to be more specific now, except to say that real progress has been made in finding the truth.

The president then came to the immunity issue:

> I have expressed to the appropriate authorities my view that no individual holding, in the past or at present, a position of major

importance in the Administration should be given immunity from
prosecution.[141]

Nixon had decided that without immunity "Dean might
be less likely to turn against me in the hope that I would grant
him an eventual pardon."[142] Dean was surprised but not cowed;
in fact, he was fighting angry. He told Fielding, "Well, the President thinks I won't talk without immunity from prosecution.
He thinks he can scare me back into the fold. But he's wrong.
I don't have any choice. It looks like the President is choosing
his team, and it's going to be me against the big guys."[143]
Haldeman and others, in retrospect, view the immunity
decision as a major tactical error. If Dean had been granted
immunity, "he wouldn't have reached so high to try to obtain
it, and Nixon would never have been dragged in."[144] The president had never believed that Dean would dare disclose "national
security matters" like the Fielding burglary or private conversations with him, which Nixon believed, were protected by executive privilege. On the morning of the seventeenth, he told
Haldeman, "I don't think Dean would go so far as to get into
any conversation he had with the President—even Dean I don't
think."[145]
Dean saw two reasons why Nixon was lining up with
Haldeman and Ehrlichman against him:

> One is that Haldeman and Ehrlichman have him by the balls so
> tight he doesn't have a choice. If that's true, nothing I do will
> make any difference. But the other possibility is that Ehrlichman
> and Haldeman have him convinced that he can run over me. If
> that's the reason, maybe a little public notice might do some
> good.[146]

On April 19, Dean released a statement that the president
was sure to understand. It concluded, ". . . [s]ome may hope
or think that I will become a scapegoat in the Watergate case.
Anyone who believes this does not know me, know the true
facts. . . ."[147]
Nixon got other bad news that day. The *Washington Post*
reported that Magruder had told the grand jury that John Dean
and John Mitchell had approved the Watergate bugging.[148] The

next day William Hundley, Mitchell's attorney, acknowledged that Mitchell had been present at three meetings in which plans to wiretap the Democrats were discussed.

Deeply concerned about Magruder's defection and aware that Dean's testimony would be far more devastating, Nixon tried to soothe Dean with a "stroking call" on April 22 wishing him a "Happy Easter" and telling him "you're still my counsel." Dean felt that there was still a "spark of hope."[149] It was quickly extinguished. Newspaper stories, discrediting Dean, and obviously planted by the White House, began to appear.

During the last days of April, Haldeman and Ehrlichman were stepping up their demands that Nixon dismiss Dean. Nixon knew that there was a problem with firing Dean outright. "If you break it off with him, then he could go out and say 'Screw the _____.'"[150] The president was still trying to find some way of dumping Dean without arousing his ire even more. Gradually, however, he realized that he could only fire Dean if he fired Haldeman and Ehrlichman. As public suspicion of the president's involvement grew almost daily, the continued presence of Haldeman and Ehrlichman only damaged him further.

On April 30, President Nixon, in a televised address to the nation, announced the resignations of Haldeman, Ehrlichman, Kleindeinst, and Dean. Nixon characterized Haldeman and Ehrlichman as "two of the finest public servants it has ever been my privilege to know" and stated their resignations carried "no implication whatever of personal wrongdoing." Kleindeinst, he said, had "no personal involvement in the matter."[151] The president offered no such disclaimer for Dean, strongly implying that he was deeply involved.

The "core" had been reduced to one.

1.8 Could It Have Ended Differently?

The coverup collapsed because the president simply did not have the means to ensure the silence of the conspirators in the face of the pressures originally produced by Sirica to defect. George Higgins, in his usual graphic style, argues that nobody "with an overriding disinclination to use a revolver" could have held the coverup together. This restraint

> . . . made participation in the coverup a volitional matter. Just
> another damned option that you had. . . . Okay, so long as no-
> body came along with something that you feared more than you
> cherished what you had, e.g., twenty or thirty years in jail. The
> Mob's men don't take money for their families, and the prepaid
> services of counsel, just because they're so grateful for the lar-
> gesse that they cheerfully undertake to do five to seven as a
> spontaneous gesture of fraternal solidarity: they do it, and keep
> their mouths shut, because if they don't, they'll wind up in the
> harbor with a couple in the head. That kind of certitude makes
> a man a whole lot more tractable, reliable and patient if the cash
> is late one month, or less than he'd been led to expect or had
> demanded.[152]

2

Madness would have had to prevail at the White House if the resignations [of Richardson and Ruckelshaus] were either intended from the first or invited at the last. They were invited.

John Osborne,
The Fifth Year of the Nixon Watch

I felt I had no other option than to act as I did.

Richard Nixon, *RN*

The question of what I would do, I think, was unclear from his [Nixon's] perspective up to the point on Saturday afternoon when I came in to see him.

Elliot Richardson,
news conference, October 23, 1973

The Saturday Night Massacre Game

2.1 Cox's Appointment to the Court of Appeals Decision

By late April 1973, the Watergate coverup began to disintegrate. President Nixon faced disclosures, charges and countercharges related to Watergate and demands from political leaders, the legal profession, and the press for the establishment of a Watergate prosecutor independent of the Justice Department.[1] In an attempt to counter this and halt the erosion of public confidence in his integrity, Nixon announced in his April 30 address that "new information" concerning the involvement of aides in the Watergate affair had come to his attention. He accepted formal responsibility (but eschewed blame) for the break-in and coverup. After revealing the "resignations" of H. R. Haldeman, John Ehrlichman, John Dean, and Attorney General Richard Kleindeinst, he announced the nomination of Secretary of Defense Elliot Richardson as the new attorney general. Richardson would have "absolute authority" on all decisions relating to Watergate prosecutions and would also have the authority to appoint a "supervising special prosecutor."[2]

The appointment of a special prosecutor immediately became the central issue in the Senate Judiciary Committee's consideration of Richardson's confirmation. Several senators, including Mansfield, Byrd, Tunney, and Kennedy, threatened to withhold confirmation unless Richardson agreed *in advance* to name a special prosecutor and to provide institutional safeguards for his independence. Richardson balked, at first suggesting the appointment of an assistant attorney general to handle Watergate matters. This proved unacceptable to eight of 16 committee members (Eastland, Ervin, Bayh, Tunney, Stevenson, Byrd, Cook, and Kennedy). Finally, after two weeks of resisting, Richardson capitulated. On May 17 he presented formal guidelines (which became law as Justice Department regulations) defining the special prosecutor's role and guaranteeing his independence. The special prosecutor would have full authority to investigate members of the White House staff and presidential appointees and to contest in court all claims of privilege by the Nixon administration. The special prosecutor alone would determine "to what extent he will inform or consult with the attorney general about the conduct of his duties and responsibilities"; he would report to the public periodically on the progress of his work and present a final report to Congress. Finally, the special prosecutor could only be fired by the attorney general for "extraordinary improprieties."[3]

The following day Richardson named Archibald Cox, a Harvard law professor who had been Richardson's teacher and solicitor general under Presidents Kennedy and Johnson, as the Watergate special prosecutor. Both men appeared before the committee on May 21; Cox pledged he would not "shield anybody and did not intend to be intimidated by anybody" in conducting an independent and thorough investigation of Watergate. Cox expressed complete satisfaction that Richardson's proposed guidelines gave him all the freedom he needed to investigate federal crime "wherever the trail may lead."[4] Evidently satisfied with Cox's testimony, the Judiciary Committee unanimously recommended Richardson's confirmation and the Senate confirmed him as attorney general on May 23 by a vote of 82 to 3.

Beginning in late April and culminating in his June appearance before the Ervin Committee, John Dean had alleged a deliberate and elaborate coverup of the Watergate affair. Dean had accused the president of permitting the coverup to continue even after Dean had informed him of its extent. Dean further alleged that Nixon had discussed with him the possibility of executive clemency for some of the Watergate conspirators and hush money payments to maintain the coverup. During this period, the main line of Nixon's defense was that the whole Watergate matter came down to the question of "Who's lying?" Was the president of the United States or was a former counsel who admitted his part in an obstruction of justice? Fred Thompson, minority counsel to the Ervin Committee, has described the general form of "Who's lying?" cases:

> The pattern was . . . one of matching the word of someone on
> the inside who had decided to cleanse his soul, usually receiving
> immunity from prosecution for his action, against the word of
> those he accused, who insist that their accuser is a new Judas
> seeking to save his own skin.[5]

A possible key to resolve the question of who was lying
was revealed on July 12 when Alexander Butterfield, a little-
known former staff assistant to H. R. Haldeman, told the Ervin
committee of the existence of an extensive White House taping
system. The special prosecutor, recognizing that the tapes represented the best available evidence to resolve questions of the
president's participation in the coverup and John Dean's credibility as a witness, wrote the president requesting the tapes of
nine presidential conversations, memoranda, and other documents. Two days later, having received no reply, Cox repeated
his request. On July 23, the reply came. The president would
not surrender the tapes either to the special prosecutor or to the
Ervin Committee, which had requested tapes of five conversations.
The president stated that he based his refusal on the constitutional principles of separation of powers and "executive privilege." Finding himself at an impasse, Cox subpoenaed the nine
tapes; the Ervin Committee subpoenaed five.

Cox believed that moving the tapes issue into the courts
was fraught with great danger:

> A protracted court fight would mean the possibility that the Pres-
> ident's position would be upheld and the evidence lost forever.
> And there was a greater danger, the possibility that Nixon would
> defy a subpoena and the courts would lack the courage to enforce
> it. Judge Sirica might find the subpoena faulty, or simply unwise,
> and refuse to enforce it. Or the appellate court might do the same.
> Or the Supreme Court might find a way to dodge the question,
> which would be worse than losing on the merits.[6]

As expected, President Nixon, on July 26, rejected the
two subpoenas and both the Ervin committee and the special
prosecutor moved the tapes issue into the courts for the first

time. Cox obtained a show-cause order from Judge Sirica directing the president to explain why he should not be compelled to release the tapes.

That same day Deputy White House Press Secretary Gerald Warren stated that President Nixon would abide by a "definitive decision of the highest court."[7] Some interpreted this remark as an implicit threat that the president was prepared to defy the judiciary should it rule against him. This interpretation was given credence on August 22 when Charles Alan Wright, the president's attorney, in oral arguments before Judge Sirica, claimed executive privilege was absolute and that the president was "beyond the process of any court." Wright argued that the only remedy found in the Constitution for the abuse of executive privilege was impeachment. When questioned by Judge Sirica concerning the president's reaction to an order to surrender the tapes to Sirica himself, Wright answered that the president felt that such an order would be "inappropriate."[8] The president at a news conference that day endorsed Warren's formulation but neither he nor other White House spokesmen would expand on the original statement.

A week later, on August 29, Judge Sirica ordered the president to turn over the nine subpoenaed tapes for *in camera* review. Sirica's decision was an attempt to walk the middle ground. On the one hand, he refused to rule on the general question of executive privilege (as sought by the president); on the other, he refused to turn the tapes directly over to the grand jury (as sought by Cox).

The White House immediately rejected the order, noting that the president's attorneys were considering an appeal or "how otherwise to sustain the President's position."[9] This phrase seemed to suggest, contrary to the Warren statement, that President Nixon might simply choose to defy Judge Sirica rather than risk the Supreme Court's reaching a "definitive" decision. The next day, however, the White House announced it would appeal Sirica's decision to the Court of Appeals in the District of Columbia. The president had apparently opted for a protracted legal confrontation which would probably be resolved in a landmark Supreme Court decision. However, there were indications that the president had other plans. Thus, *Newsweek* reported that the decision to appeal

> . . . may be little more than the opening feint in a protracted
> strategy of delay designed to prevent a final decision in the Su-
> preme Court until the President feels he has got his shattered
> majority back together again. At that point, White House sources
> said, Mr. Nixon would be prepared openly to defy anything short
> of a unanimous or near-unanimous Supreme Court ruling. . . .[10]

The Court of Appeals heard oral arguments by Wright
and Cox on September 11. Wright again challenged the judiciary's authority to rule on the matter of executive privilege, and
he again suggested that Nixon might not heed an adverse judicial
decision. "The tradition is very strong that judges should have
the last word on the production of evidence," he said, "but in
a government organized as ours is, there are times when that
simply cannot be the case." Finally, Wright urged the judges to
avoid "an aura of confrontation" that would result from a judicial order for Nixon to produce the tapes. He proposed that
the court merely "suggest what it feels should be done" and
rely on the president's "good judgment" to do what was right.[11]
   This threat to defy the court was not lost on the judges.
On September 13 the seven judges who heard the case unanimously adopted a memorandum urging an out-of-court compromise. They recommended that portions of the recordings be
examined by Cox, Wright, and the president or "his delegate,"
who would jointly decide which parts could be properly released
to the grand jury. The judges ordered Cox and the White House
to present their decision to the court by September 20. The
court, in suggesting a nonjudicial resolution of the issue, was
drawing back from "the abyss . . . of a constitutional
apocalypse."[12]
   Cox immediately expressed his willingness to "pursue the
Court of Appeals' suggestion to a mutually satisfactory conclusion."[13] The White House said nothing publicly about the proposal. However, in a brief filed before the court on September
19, Wright repeated his hard line on the tapes, arguing that "the
President has not delegated to the special prosecutor, and will
not abrogate his constitutional duties and prerogatives."[14] Given
the president's adamance, it was not surprising that on Septem-

ber 20 Cox and Wright informed the court that they were unable
to reach a compromise.[15]

On October 12, by a vote of 5 to 2, the appeals court
upheld Judge Sirica's order. Like Sirica, the majority based its
decision on very narrow legal grounds and viewed its decision
as limited in its impact. The two dissenters, George MacKinnon
and Malcolm Wilkey, both Nixon appointees, presented lengthy
opinions espousing the view that executive privilege was absolute and was to be exercised at the sole discretion of the president.[16] (Two judges, both considered members of the appeals
court's conservative wing, Roger Robb, a Nixon appointee, and
Edward Tamm disqualified themselves.) The court declared that
for the president to be permitted to decide what information he
must surrender would be "an invitation to refashion the Constitution. . . . Though the President is elected by nationwide
ballot and is often said to represent all the people, he does not
embody the nation's sovereignty. He is not above the law's
commands."[17]

The Court of Appeals' decision justified Cox's strategy
of presenting the judges an opportunity to avoid a crisis by
focusing on the uniqueness of the case. As he put it, a decision
against President Nixon "would set only a narrow but important
precedent which would reaffirm the principle that in the United
States no man is above the law."[18] By contrast, the White House
strategy gave the court only two choices: issue a broad ruling
that recognized an absolute "executive privilege" or concede
it had no legal jurisdiction over the question, which directly
threatened the judiciary's constitutional position as a coequal
branch.

The court stayed its order until October 19 to permit the
president to appeal to the Supreme Court. Still, the Court of
Appeals majority voiced the hope that the president and Cox
might mutually decide what portions of the tapes should be
turned over to the grand jury.   -

Thus, after October 13, President Nixon apparently had
three strategies available to him:

1. Comply with the Court of Appeals decision.
2. Defy the Court of Appeals.
3. Appeal to the Supreme Court.

Compliance with the Court of Appeals decision meant he would have to release damaging evidence relating to his participation in the Watergate coverup as well as his attempt to misuse federal agencies for partisan political purposes. Nixon had listened to the tapes on June 4, 1973 and over the weekend of September 28 and 29, 1973 and was aware of the harmful evidence that at least some of them contained. Since the tapes corroborated John Dean's testimony, not only would his versions of his conversations with the president be established but also his accounts of his unrecorded discussions with Haldeman, Ehrlichman, and Mitchell would be accorded greater weight. This posed a potentially serious problem for the president because if sufficient evidence were gathered against his three closest associates, they might be induced to testify against him.

The tape of March 21, 1973 presented the greatest threat to the president. Nixon had grounded his public case on his conversation with Dean that day, claiming that it was only then that he was informed of the details of the coverup. But, in fact, the tape showed this claim to be false; the president praised Dean for the success of his coverup "plan":

> [I have] . . . no doubts about the right plan before election. You handled it just right. You contained it. Now after the election we've got to have another plan.[19]

Dean had charged the president with ordering money to be paid to E. Howard Hunt to remain silent. The president contended that he firmly rejected Hunt's blackmail, telling Dean: "It would be wrong." But the tapes showed the president returning to the subject of the hush money repeatedly, finally asking Dean: "Would you agree that that's the prime thing you'd better damn well get that done?"[20] The March 21 tape directly tied President Nixon to a criminal obstruction of justice. (On June 4, after listening to the March 21 tape, Nixon stated to White House Chief of Staff Alexander Haig, "We do know we have one problem. It's that damn conversation of March twenty-first.")[21]

As damaging to the president as the content of six of the subpoenaed tapes were, the revelation that two tapes were "missing" (never recorded), and another partially erased, might be even worse. Two conversations Nixon had on June 20, 1972, one with Mitchell (never recorded) and the other with Haldeman and Ehrlichman (with the now-famous 18½ minute gap) could have established the four men's knowlege of illegal activity only three days after the break-in. The April 15 tape (never recorded, machine malfunction) could have established the president's efforts to set Dean up as a scapegoat. Although there remains much mystery surrounding the three tapes, two assumptions appear justified. The substance of the tapes was damning to the president. Also, the tapes were "lost" or erased by the president himself, or at his behest or with his knowledge. Even if there were innocent explanations, the president probably realized that they would be difficult for anyone to accept.

Outright defiance of the Court of Appeals would force the special prosecutor to request a contempt of court citation against the president; Judge Sirica would likely issue the citation (as he was prepared to do on October 23). Defiance would precipitate a constitutional confrontation between the president and judiciary and probably lead a reluctant Congress into impeachment proceedings.

However, if the president defied the judiciary it would be preferable for him to defy a split Court of Appeals than to defy the Supreme Court (should the president appeal and lose). Defiance of the nation's highest court would almost certainly lead to the initiation of an impeachment inquiry and probably result in impeachment itself. This expectation was expressed by public figures who spanned the political spectrum: Nixon's own chief domestic affairs advisor, Melvin Laird, Senate Minority Whip Robert Griffin, conservative columnist William Buckley; and Senators Kennedy, Brooke, and Ervin.[22] Senator Kennedy stated on the floor of the Senate, "If President Nixon defied a Supreme Court order to turn over the tapes, a responsible Congress would be left no recourse but to exercise its power of impeachment."[23]

The alternative of appealing to the Supreme Court presented the president with both great dangers and great opportunities. If the Supreme Court ruled against him, Nixon would have faced two distasteful outcomes. If he refused to comply, he was inviting impeachment, as we have seen. If he complied, he would face the same problem he would if he complied with the lower court ruling. However, if the Supreme Court ruled in his favor, the president would not only be exonerated but could emerge in a far stronger position.

President Nixon undoubtedly hoped that, in the event of an appeal, the court would make a "political" decision and thereby avert a constitutional crisis by ruling in his favor.[24] To pressure the court, the White House, through high administration officials and Republican leaders in Congress, indicated that the president had decided to defy any adverse Supreme Court decision, thus putting the onus of precipitating a constitutional crisis on the court.[25]

It was almost universally expected that the president would appeal. It was reported that Charles Alan Wright, among others, was absolutely certain that the court would either rule in the president's favor or produce an "indefinitive" adverse decision. However, after the Court of Appeals decision, Wright apparently began to reevaluate his earlier assessment. Appealing to the Supreme Court would either provide President Nixon with his best possible outcome if he won, or it might leave him with his worst outcome if he lost. The appellate court decision apparently seemed to the president's advisors to augur the worst.

All of these choices were unpalatable to Nixon. The president felt that the situation was "intolerable," that he was being "worn down, trapped and paralyzed."[26] The Cox investigations were getting too close to the White House on too many matters. The special prosecutor was investigating far more than "Watergate." He was inquiring into the "Plumbers," the 1969–71 wiretap program, illegal campaign contributions, the ITT antitrust settlement, "dirty tricks," and the Hughes' contribution— in short, the "White House horrors." Nixon must have been deeply concerned with Cox's success in striking deals with mid-level Watergate figures (LaRue, Magruder, Segretti) in return for testifying against other, "higher," members of the criminal hierarchy. Cox was using the classic prosecutorial strategy of "dealing up" that had recently been used so successfully in amassing evidence against Spiro Agnew.[27] Cox was publicly reported to have had evidence that would lead to "sensational indictments" against some of the president's closest associates:

Mitchell, Colson, Haldeman, Ehrlichman and Kleindeinst. Indeed, Nixon believed that Cox was about to indict him.[28]

Nixon deeply regretted that he had agreed to Cox's selection. The president was convinced that Cox was a "partisan zealot," a liberal Kennedy Democrat out to get him.[29] Nixon and his aides believed that the mere existence of a special prosecution force and the announced scope of its investigation were having a divisive and paralyzing effect on the administration and the nation.[30]

For these reasons, the president decided to make what he liked to call "the big play"—a bold, dramatic move that would take a crisis and turn it to his advantage.[31] He decided to "fire Cox and return the Watergate investigation to the Justice Department." He would turn over third-person summaries instead of transcripts of the subpoenaed tapes.[32]

2.2 Six Days in October: Monday October 15 to Thursday October 18

On Monday morning, October 15, Attorney General Richardson was summoned to the White House where he met with White House Chief of Staff, Alexander Haig, and the president's chief Watergate lawyer, Fred Buzhardt. The two informed Richardson that the president would neither appeal the court ruling nor obey it. Rather, he would submit third-person summaries of the tapes and then dismiss Cox. Richardson argued that firing Cox would be disastrous and indicated he might resign if ordered to do so.[33]

Cox's firing, coupled with Richardson's resignation, would have resulted in a public outcry and significant opposition in Congress (as actually occurred the following Saturday). Richardson was originally selected attorney general because he was the only reliable and "clean" high administration official President Nixon could find to oversee the Watergate investigation. During the almost seven months of his tenure, he was the administration's symbol of integrity. His reputation for rectitude and propriety was enhanced by his handling of the Agnew affair, which had led to the vice president's resignation five days earlier.

Since the president needed Richardson's support in any

confrontation with Cox, Cox's firing was dropped from the discussion. The three men then examined other alternatives, including a third-party review to authenticate the tape summaries.

On the afternoon of the fifteenth Haig told Richardson that the president had agreed to a third-party review by Senator John Stennis. The choice of Senator Stennis was ingenious. Stennis, a Democrat, was President Nixon's strongest Senate supporter. On April 27, 1973 he publicly urged the president to "tough out" Watergate. Also, Stennis had a reputation for rising above principle in the interests of "national security" (presumably a major justification for excising material from any tape summary). However, Senator Stennis was a demigod in Washington, a Senate baron. President Nixon clearly was counting on senatorial courtesy toward Stennis to immobilize that body in any confrontation with Cox; a rejection of Stennis by Cox would be seen as an insult to the Senate itself.

Cox would have to agree to refrain from seeking further evidence from the White House. "This is it."[34] Additionally, Richardson would have to fire Cox if he balked at the proposal. Richardson expressed his support of the Stennis review but did not commit himself to fire Cox. He agreed to meet with Cox to try to persuade him to accept the proposal.[35]

The president had won much in Richardson's endorsement of the so-called "Stennis compromise." He would be releasing narrative summaries prepared exclusively by the White House and verified by an outspoken supporter of the president instead of submitting verbatim transcripts authenticated by the special prosecutor, as ordered by the Court of Appeals.

That evening Richardson presented the White House proposal to Cox, who expressed reservations but agreed to consider it.[36] Tuesday morning they continued the discussion. Richardson warned Cox that the White House had set a Friday deadline for them to reach an agreement; if they did not, "the consequences will be very serious for both of us" (an implicit warning that the president might fire Cox).[37] Cox believed that the concern with the appellate court's Friday deadline was a facade since the court would have granted an extension. The only reasonable explanation that Richardson offered was the president's desire to settle the tapes issue quickly because of the Middle East war.[38] Cox realized that he was not being offered a compromise, that the president was playing a very different game: "I had already figured out for myself that if I were the President and I were going to disobey a court decision, I would not take it to the Supreme Court."[39] Cox suggested that Richardson put the proposal in writing.

Wednesday afternoon, Richardson dispatched the proposal (with White House revisions) to Cox. Absent from the revised draft was any discussion of future access to evidence.[40] Either Richardson misunderstood the White House omission or, "understanding it perfectly, helped perpetuate confusion between Cox and the White House in the hope that other elements of a bargain could be struck first and the confusion cleared up afterward."[41] When Richardson called for Cox's reply, the special prosecutor informed him that he would respond in writing. (He was building a case if a showdown came.)

Expecting such a showdown, Cox's staff, late Wednesday evening, began feverish negotiations with John Dean whom they considered a "significant piece of ammunition . . . for any confrontation with the President."[42] Thursday afternoon, Dean and the prosecutors agreed to a one-count plea that would relieve Dean of potential criminal liability for all other Watergate misdeeds except perjury. The perjury exception would signal to the president that Dean was sticking to his account of the coverup at the peril of criminal sanctions.[43]

Thursday afternoon Cox replied to Richardson, expressing his willingness to compromise on the court ruling. He accepted the concept of a nonjudicial means of providing an accurate record of the subpoenaed tapes' contents *without* his participation—a significant departure from what he had won in the courts. Apparently, Cox was willing to go this far since he was concerned that the Supreme Court would rule against him. Nonetheless, Cox made it clear that the proposal was unacceptable in its present form, that a great deal remained to be negotiated. He listed eleven "highly important" points which needed clarification or revision before he could agree to it. Finally, Cox wrote, "You appointed me and I pledged [to the Senate] that I would not be turned aside. Any solution I can accept must be such to command conviction that I am adhering to that pledge.''[44] He was warning Richardson that in any confrontation with the president, Richardson could not side with the president (or, indeed, remain "neutral") with impunity.

Thursday evening, Richardson met with Haig and Buzhardt, who were joined by Charles Alan Wright and Leonard Garment. All but Richardson viewed Cox's reply as tantamount to a complete rejection of the proposal. The White House people agreed that Cox should be fired if he did not accept the plan as presented to him on Wednesday. Richardson apparently indicated that he could "live with" Cox's voluntary resignation but that he could not fire him for refusing the Stennis plan.[45] Haig, Buzhardt, Wright, and Garment were confident that the president could persuade the public of the reasonableness of such an action. Richardson, believing that Cox would not accept the White House plan, told Wright that, since he was so strongly in favor of the proposal, he should negotiate with Cox. (Until Friday evening, after the White House had irrevocably acted, Richardson had no contact with Cox; the president, through Wright, "negotiated" directly with the special prosecutor.) Wright later telephoned Cox, who recalls Wright's conversation as "decidedly nasty" and "designed to elicit rejection." According to Cox, Wright's opening conversational gambit was, "Here are some conditions you can't accept.''[46] After their conversation, both men wrote each other letters of clarification. In his, Wright informed Cox that certain features of the proposal were nonnegotiable, among these, the prohibition on further access. Wright closed his letter remarking that if Cox thought that there was "any purpose in our talking further, my associates and I stand ready to do so. If not we will have to follow the course of action that we think is in the best interests of the country.''[47] Wright's letter, rather than spelling out the conditions of compromise, seemed designed to end negotiations.

2.3 Richardson-Cox Game as Perceived by the White House
The Players and Their Strategies

Late Thursday evening, Haig, Buzhardt and Nixon discussed how best to be rid of Cox and to resolve the question of future access to evidentiary material. White House lawyers had analyzed Cox's possible reactions to the proposal Richardson had presented and had concluded that the special prosecutor had three choices:

1. "he could accept the Stennis compromise;"
2. "he could reject it and do nothing;"
3. "he could reject it and resign."[48]

Elliot Richardson, the other figure whose actions were critical to the White House, could either:

1. Resign as attorney general (thus, at least implicitly, support Cox).
2. Remain as attorney general (thus, at least implicitly, support the president).

The White House's perception of the choices available to Richardson and Cox are presented in the (partial) game tree in Figure 2.1. The game tree, or the representation of the game in *extensive* form, depicts the step-by-step sequence of moves. The game tree shows that Cox had two choices open to him and, depending on his decision, there were four possible choices open to Richardson. That is, before Cox chose, any of the four outcomes could occur.

The game presented in Figures 2.1, 2.2 and 2.3 is a "game in the head." That is, the strategies, the outcomes and the players' rankings of the outcomes are attributed by the White House to Richardson and Cox.

If Cox had accepted the proposal, the entire game would have ended. (Strictly speaking, if Cox accepted there would have been no game.) The president would have succeeded in thwarting the investigation and prosecution of Watergate crimes, particularly concerning his and his closest aides' involvement. The president would have submitted edited third-person summaries of the nine taped conversations but no subpoenaed papers, memoranda, or other documents. There is little doubt that the summaries would have answered the question "Who's lying?" in terms favorable to the president or would be so ambiguous that no firm conclusions could be drawn.

Cox's acquiescence would represent a de facto pardon for present and future Watergate defendants because they could

FIGURE 2.1
PARTIAL GAME TREE OF PERCEIVED RICHARDSON-COX GAME

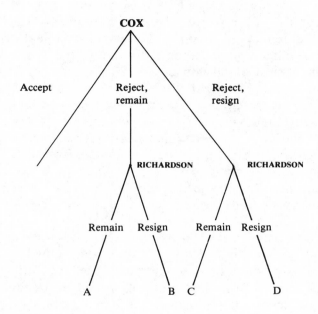

NOTE: The "accept" outcome is not considered a "true" outcome since it is unnecessary
       for Richardson to have made a choice.

argue that they were denied due process since potentially ex-
culpatory evidence was withheld from them. Cox's acceptance
would guarantee that there would be little or no opposition to
the proposal. Acceptance of the proposal was clearly Special
Prosecutor Cox's worst choice. He would be emasculating the
entire Watergate investigation and prosecution. He would be
violating his pledges given to the Senate to challenge the president in court, if warranted. He would be accepting far less than
he won from the Court of Appeals, which had ruled that Cox
would "inspect" and be "heard" on any presidential claims of
privilege.

    However, Cox and his staff, although seriously weak-
ened, would remain "partisan vipers . . . in our bosom."[49] The

president and his aides feared that they could never fully recover from the demoralizing effects of the Watergate scandals if the Watergate Special Prosecution Force were allowed to continue.[50]

Attorney General Richardson would have been freed from his conflict of loyalties to the president on one hand and to Cox and the Senate on the other. He would remain attorney general and keep his reputation for honor and integrity intact; his image as the "great compromiser" would be enhanced, his political prospects bright. This is Richardson's most preferred outcome.

This outcome was considered most unlikely by Haig, Buzhardt, and Nixon. They had concluded that Cox would reject the proposal. Cox's letter that afternoon *was*, as far as the president's aims were concerned, a complete rejection. Wright's reponse was intended to signal Cox that the White House preferred, indeed welcomed, rejection. Thus, the "accept" outcome is not considered a true outcome of the game.

The Outcomes and Their Rankings by the Players

If Cox rejected the "Stennis compromise" and then resigned in protest, there would have been opposition to the proposal, at least from the "radicals" in the House and Senate and from elements of the media. Cox's resignation would have removed a constant and severe source of irritation and danger to the president, particularly if, as expected, Cox's staff would also resign. The investigation and prosecution would, at the least, be seriously delayed, for a new group of prosecutors would have to become familiar with the case.

If Cox resigned and Richardson remained attorney general (outcome C in Figure 2.1), Cox would have been isolated in his rejection of the proposal. The president would have probably either requested the vacating of the Court of Appeals ruling or would have presented the "compromise" to Judge Sirica. Richardson would have come under fire for supporting a proposal that clearly violated the thrust of the Court of Appeals decision.

If Richardson resigned in support of Cox (outcome D), the president would have faced strong opposition, perhaps culminating in the opening of an impeachment inquiry. At the very least, the president's next nominee for attorney general would not be confirmed unless another special prosecutor was appointed. Richardson's presidential aspirations would have been severely hampered; Richard Nixon would never forgive Richardson's act of disloyalty and, although politically weakened, could successfully block Richardson's rise within the Republican party.

If Cox rejected the proposal, remained, and "did nothing" (that is, "waited until further justification developed for a resumption of his needs should they have developed"[51]) and Richardson remained (outcome A), the White House had concluded that Cox, finding himself opposed by Richardson and the president, would soon resign.[52]

These conflicting considerations are now combined into a (White House-perceived) ranking of the four outcomes by Cox and Richardson.

Haig, Buzhardt, and Nixon believed that whatever strategy Cox might choose, Richardson would prefer to remain (outcomes A and C); hence (A-C,D-B). Despite his reputation for rectitude, Richardson was seen by some as a man whose commitment to principle was sometimes overcome by ambition. Richard Nixon had reason to hold this view. As Nixon's undersecretary of state, Richardson quietly endured the secret bombing and then the open invasion of Cambodia (although it was widely rumored that he objected to these actions). As secretary of health, education and welfare, Richardson reversed his own and his department's policies on school desegregation and welfare reform when these policies were publicly repudiated by the White House. Finally, as defense secretary his acquiescence—in fact, strong support—of the 1972 bombing of Hanoi "must have convinced his boss that whatever the provocation, he would never resign."[53] By his own admission, he was "loyal," a "team player."[54]

The White House further believed that Richardson would prefer Cox to resign (C), since it would free him from his obligation to Cox and the Senate; hence (C,A). Finally, the White House believed that Richardson would resign only if the opposition generated by a Cox resignation made his remaining attorney general totally untenable; hence (D,B).

Thus, the White House presumed that Richardson's ranking of the four outcomes, (from best to worst) defined by his and Cox's two strategies (where subscript, R, represents Richardson and subscript, C, represents Cox), was

C. Remain$_R$/Reject, resign$_C$;

A. Remain$_R$/Reject, remain$_C$;

D. Resign$_R$/Reject, resign$_C$;

B. Resign$_R$/Reject, remain$_C$.

The White House believed that if he were to resign (C or D), Cox would prefer that Attorney General Richardson resign also (D). Richardson's resignation would preclude the White House from portraying the special prosecutor as an obstructionist; hence (D,C). The White House also believed that if Richardson remained (A or C), Cox would prefer to resign (C) rather than remain (A), since both the White House and Richardson would be lined up against him. Cox would be free to go public with his objections to the proposal; hence (C,A). Richardson resigning while the special prosecutor remained (B) is considered to be Cox's worst outcome since he would probably prefer to deal with a known quantity as attorney general.

Thus, the president presumed that Cox's ranking of the four outcomes (from best to worst), defined by Richardson's and Cox's two strategies, was:

D. Reject, resign$_C$/Resign$_R$;

C. Reject, resign$_C$/Remain$_R$;

A. Reject, remain$_C$/Remain$_R$;

B. Reject, remain$_C$/Resign$_R$.

If the best outcome for each player is represented by "4," second-best by "3," and so on, the rankings of the four outcomes in the Figure 2.1 game tree are shown as the endpoints of the four lower branches in the game tree in Figure 2.2 (read from top to bottom). The matrix, or *normal-form*, representation of this game is presented in Figure 2.3. Here Cox has two strategies (that is, to reject and resign or to reject and remain) and Richardson has four strategies. This is so because each of Richardson's two original strategies (that is, to resign or to remain)

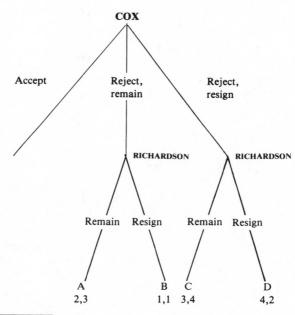

FIGURE 2.2
GAME TREE OF PERCEIVED RICHARDSON-COX GAME

NOTE: x, y = Cox, Richardson.

are contingent on Cox's strategy choice, which yields 2 × 2 = 4 strategies for Richardson.

The payoffs in Figure 2.3 can be derived from the payoffs in Figure 2.2. For example, assume that Cox chooses his "reject and resign" strategy and Richardson chooses "resign if Cox resigns, remain if Cox remains" strategy (column 4). The choices of these strategies yields the payoff (4,2) associated with the reject, resign$_C$/resign$_R$ outcome in the game tree in Figure 2.2.

Analysis of the "Game in the Head"

The White House believed that Richardson's "remain" strategy was strictly *dominant*, that Richardson preferred to remain regardless of Cox's strategy choice. His decision to remain would result in his best or second-best outcome. The White House believed that Cox would so rank the outcomes that he

FIGURE 2.3
NORMAL-FORM OF PERCEIVED RICHARDSON-COX GAME

RICHARDSON

	Remain regardless	Resign regardless	Resign if Cox remains, remain if Cox resigns	Resign if Cox resigns, remain if Cox remains
COX Reject, remain	A. 2,3	B. 1,1	E. 1,1	F. 2,3
Reject, resign	C. (3,4)	D. 4,2	G. 3,4	H. 4,2

Richardson has a dominant strategy.

Cox has a dominant strategy.

NOTE: 1. x, y = Cox, Richardson.
       2. The circled outcome is in equilibrium; it is the rational outcome.

too would have a dominant strategy: to resign. Cox's decision to resign would guarantee at least his second-best outcome.

The choice of dominant strategies by each of the players would result in outcome C, giving Richardson his best outcome and Cox his second best. Furthermore, outcome C would have been the best outcome for the president. According to Alexander Haig, "We thought—and frankly we hoped—that he [Cox] would resign."[55]

Although Cox would be gone, the question of future access remained. The president had concluded that including a prohibition on future access in the proposal would make Cox unmistakably aware of his determination. Cox, realizing the futility of his efforts, would resign in protest.[56] The White House believed that this would "pose no problems" for Richardson, who, freed of his obligation to Cox and the Senate, would remain.[57]

The three men were aware, nonetheless, of the dangers of Cox's remaining and openly defying the president.[58] In that case, the president might have to order Richardson to fire Cox, possibly precipitating Richardson's resignation. But they were convinced that they could induce Cox to resign and that Richardson would remain. Their actions the next day were designed to ensure Cox's resignation. Meanwhile, Richardson, fearing that the president would order Cox fired, drafted a letter to the president outlining the reasons why he would then feel compelled to resign.

2.4 Six Days in October:
Friday October 19 and Saturday October 20

Friday morning Cox appeared in Judge Sirica's court to hear John Dean's guilty plea. Dean's unexpected action "set the town on edge."[59] The universal question was, "What other surprises might Cox have in store?" (One of the surprises that Richard Nixon felt was in store was an indictment.)[60] If Cox's intention was to cause the president to move slowly in any move against him, he was unsuccessful. Dean's plea must have convinced the president of the need to be rid of Cox immediately.

That morning, Richardson called the White House to see

if Wright had made any progress in his talks with Cox. He informed Haig that if negotiations reached an impasse, he wished an audience with the president. This was an implicit threat to resign. Shortly after, Haig called Richardson and told him a stalemate had been reached; Richardson reasserted his desire to see the president, and Haig acquiesced.

However, when Richardson arrived at the White House he was faced with a sharp change of tack. Haig suggested that "maybe we don't have to go down the road we talked about last night. Suppose we go ahead with the Stennis plan without firing Cox."[61] Richardson was shown Cox's letter and was surprised by the special prosecutor's objection to the prohibition on further access. Richardson pointed out that he had never asked Cox to make such a promise; he insisted that Wright send Cox another letter explaining that this limitation was never part of the proposal. That letter, delivered later that day, stated that the prohibition applied only to "private Presidential papers and meetings." Wright pointed out that the clarification was only "in the interest of historical accuracy" and "not to reopen discussion." On the contrary, he wrote that "further discussions between us seeking to resolve this matter by compromise would be futile."[62]

Richardson, Haig, Buzhardt, and presidential aide Leonard Garment went on to discuss means of implementing the Stennis proposal and for preventing, or at least containing, future demands by the special prosecutor for presidential tapes and documents. They decided to "forget about Cox and concentrate on persuading Sirica," an "end-run" tactic that Richardson again proposed the following day.[63]

During the course of the conversation, the prohibition on access again was linked to the Stennis proposal. Exactly how this transpired and what Richardson's position was is subject to dispute between Richardson and the White House participants. According to Buzhardt and Garment, Richardson strongly agreed that the Stennis compromise was a good one and suggested that in future cases Cox could be ordered not to seek access to presidential tapes and files. To the others in the meeting, it appeared that Richardson was "coming on board" on the access question.[64] To Richardson, this point about ordering Cox not to demand more tapes was raised as a tactic for the future.

Richardson claims he said nothing about what he might do if the prohibition were ordered or even gave "any clear indication of my attitude on this."[65]

Why did Richardson remain silent on such a vital issue? One explanation, suggested by his previous behavior, is that he realized that the president was set on ridding himself of Cox. If Cox were fired for any reason, he would have to resign. But if Cox could be maneuvered to resign, he might be able to remain.

Significantly, all accounts agree that Richardson preferred the opinion that Cox would resign if faced with an outright prohibition on future access. This confirmed the president's analysis of the evening before, an evaluation probably based, in part, on Cox's previous behavior. For example, in 1952, President Truman granted coal miners a far larger wage increase than that recommended by his own Wage Stabilization Board. The increase was widely written off as an understandable favor for a friendly client. However, as head of the Wage Stabilization Board, Cox resigned in protest over what he felt was the unwarranted increase.

Whatever Richardson's intent, his behavior that afternoon left the "impression among the president's people that Richardson would go along with . . . an order to Cox to halt his demands for presidential evidence."[66]

Richardson claims that he later phoned Haig and reiterated his position that the Stennis compromise was reasonable but that it should not be coupled with a restriction on Cox's freedom of action. Richardson further indicated that he now believed that Cox would not be induced to resign by this device. The president's men contend that Richardson never clearly objected to the proposal that afternoon. In any event, it was too late. Confronted with a midnight deadline for a Supreme Court appeal, Nixon, Haig, and Buzhardt were moving quickly to effectuate the plan.

As noted, Cox's Thursday letter had implicitly warned the White House that he would not voluntarily accede to his isolation. He reminded the White House that the Senate, through the Judiciary Committee, was a potential ally. Friday afternoon, the White House moved to neutralize Senate opposition to any White House actions against Cox. The first step was to cement

Senator Stennis' participation. Next, Senators Ervin and Baker, the leaders of the Senate Watergate committee, were summoned to the White House to meet with Nixon, Haig, and Wright. They persuaded the senators that the Stennis option offered a quick solution to the tapes issue demanded by the Middle East crisis. After a forty-minute meeting, the two Senators agreed to recommend the Stennis plan to the Senate Watergate committee. Cox was isolated as "the lone holdout against a presumptively reasonable deal, leaving him vulnerable to dismissal."[67] The Senators' agreement gave the White House its major claim to credibility for its plan.

By Friday evening, the president and his aides were confident that they had the deal wrapped up. Ervin, Baker, and Stennis were supporting the proposal, and they believed that Richardson would strongly support the basic proposal and would, at the least, tacitly acquiesce to the prohibition on access. They remained certain that Richardson still had a dominant strategy: remain, regardless of what Cox did.

At 7 P.M. Richardson received a call from Haig who read him a letter from the president instructing him to direct Cox "to make no further attempts by judicial means to obtain tapes, notes or memoranda of Presidential conversations."[68] Richardson gave no indication of whether or not he would issue the order. Haig assumed that Richardson was balking only at issuing the order to Cox but that he was still with the White House in supporting the entire Stennis compromise in principle. Richardson's support was the key to the plan's success: "The only way this thing can float is if Elliot's on board 100 per cent; otherwise it will sink to the bottom of the sea."[69]

At 7:30 P.M. Richardson was sending very different signals to Cox. Richardson called Cox and told him of the letter but, according to Richardson, "I . . . made it explicitly clear that I was not transmitting these instructions to him."[70] From this, Cox could reasonably presume that Richardson would back him in a showdown with the president, that is, Richardson's "remain (and at least implicitly support the president)" strategy was not dominant. But Cox and his staff were not *certain* of Richardson's support although "they thought he would [support

Cox] and his actions . . . had certainly indicated the strong likelihood that he would."[71]

At 8:15 P.M., acting on the assumption that Richardson was "on board," the White House announced the order through a press release, eliminating Richardson as an intermediary. According to Woodward and Bernstein, Haig took this action to take Richardson "off the hook." If the White House forced Richardson to issue the order himself, he might have no option but to resign.[72]

The release stated that the president had compromised with the courts and the Senate, that he was making summaries of the subpoenaed tapes available to Senator Stennis, and that Senators Ervin and Baker had agreed to this. The statement implied that the entire proposal had Richardson's support. According to Theodore White,

> The statement was, in its own terms, a masterpiece of political art—it floated on a rhetoric of conciliation, compromise and earnest good will. What it left out, flatly, was the fact that the President was *not* complying with the order of the Court of Appeals issued the previous Friday.[73]

The statement contained the implicit threat that the president would fire Cox if he did not acquiesce.

The next move was Cox's. Cox presumably reasoned that he had "the court, the law and the *Attorney General* on his side."[74] He accordingly released his own statement accusing the president of refusing to comply with the Court of Appeals decree and violating Richardson's promises to the Senate. Cox concluded that to comply with the president's order "would violate my solemn pledge to the Senate and the country to invoke judicial process to challenge exaggerated claims of executive privilege. I shall not violate my pledge."[75] He announced a press conference for 1:00 P.M. the following afternoon. The White House interpreted Cox's statement to mean that he would resign the following day.

Meanwhile, Richardson received a phone call from presidential aide Bryce Harlow to determine Richardson's reaction to the president's letter. The attorney general said he felt "shabbily treated.''[76] Haig, when told of Richardson's feelings, found this "dumbfounding.''[77] It was not until 9:00 A.M. that Richardson learned of the White House release from Cox.

Later that evening, Haig called Richardson and "angrily led him through the events of the week, reminding him that he had been party to each phase of the compromise. He had gone along with everything . . ., even the restrictions on future access.''[78] Haig also discussed initial reactions to the compromise; prominent members of both parties were favorably disposed.

The reaction to the Stennis proposal must have pleased the White House. Many of Stennis' Senate colleagues immediately voiced their confidence in him. The first reaction of the congressional leadership ranged from cautiously favorable to enthusiastic acceptance. Senate Majority Leader Mansfield, while saying he thought Cox had been granted independent powers, termed the Stennis plan "a move to avoid a constitutional confrontation." Speaker of the House Carl Albert called the proposal "interesting." Senate Minority Leader Hugh Scott said he felt "a very wise solution had been reached and a constitutional question avoided." Senator Baker called the plan "very good, totally in the best interests of the country.''[79]

Apparently convinced that he could still negotiate an agreement that would allow him to stay, Richardson again let an opportunity for a confrontation pass. Instead, he drafted a letter to the president which, although expressing his disagreement with the restriction on further access, suggested that Judge Sirica be persuaded to accept the Stennis plan (thus bypassing Cox) and that the plan could serve as a model if and when other tapes were subpoenaed. The letter was redrafted and sent to the White House early Saturday morning. The letter must have confirmed to the White House that "Richardson would squirm and fight but that in the end he would follow orders.''[80]

On Saturday morning Cox contacted Sam Dash, the chief counsel to the Ervin committee, and warned him that the loss of the support of Ervin could be fatal. Dash and committee members Daniel Inouye and Lowell Weicker then persuaded Ervin to wire the White House and insist on verbatim transcripts.

At 1:00 P.M. Cox went before the nation. He stated that he simply could not accept the president's order, since it represented "a basic change in the institutional arrangement" that was established. He listed four "insuperable" difficulties with the proposal and noted that long before the controversy over the tapes arose the White House had refused to turn over information necessary to his inquiry. Cox said he would go before the court and "seek an order to show cause why the respondent, President Nixon, should not be adjudicated guilty of contempt."[81]

The special prsecutor stated that he had no intention to resign, "No, hell—no. I'm going to go about my duties on the terms on which I assumed them."[82] Furthermore, Cox challenged Nixon's right to remove him, stating that only Richardson could. "I was appointed by the Attorney General. . . . I think there is a question whether anyone other than the Attorney General can give me any instructions that I have any legal obligation to obey."[83]

After the president's Friday night directive Cox essentially had two choices:

1. Resign and publicly attack the proposal.
2. Remain and publicly attack the proposal.

Cox's second strategy was, as we have seen, unanticipated by the White House. His "hell, no" statement simultaneously signalled its existence and its selection. Cox had decided to remain and press his case regardless of what Nixon and Richardson might subsequently do. (For the Nixon-Richardson game, see pp. 86–94.)

However, Cox needed Richardson's support to establish firmly the legitimacy of his defiance. His greatest fear was that "when push came to shove Richardson would not back him up."[84] Cox was taking no chances; in the press conference, according to Elizabeth Drew, he "had slipped the hook into Richardson and the Senate"; if he went he "intended to take their honor with him."[85]

Cox attempted to structure the strategic environment so that either President Nixon would not order Richardson to fire him or Richardson would disobey such an order. He attempted to change Richardson's evaluation of the outcomes, that is, make the "remain (at least implicitly support the president)" strategy more costly. Consequently, Cox was raising the price of the president's firing him. "Cox knew that his defiance had probably cost him his job; but if the President realized that Cox would take Richardson down with him, Nixon might have second thoughts."[86]

After Cox's press conference, the president realized that his evaluation of the strategies available to Cox had been wrong. Cox would not "remain and do nothing." The president had been playing the wrong (that is, misperceived) game. Cox had successfully induced the very game which both the president and Richardson had strived to avoid.

2.5 Saturday Night Massacre Game
The Players and Their Strategies
After Cox's press conference, President Nixon had two choices:

1. Let Cox stand in defiance, continue negotiations with him and/ or present the proposal directly to Judge Sirica.
2. Order Richardson to fire Cox immediately.

If the president ordered Richardson to fire Cox, the attorney general had four choices:

1. Fire Cox and resign.
2. Fire Cox and remain.
3. Refuse to fire Cox and resign.
4. Refuse to fire Cox and remain.

If the president let Cox stand in defiance, Richardson would be faced with two alternatives:

1. Remain as attorney general and continue efforts at negotiation.
2. Resign.

The president's and Richardson's choices are represented in the game tree in Figure 2.4 It shows that Nixon had two choices open to him, and—depending on his choice—there were six choices open to Richardson. That is, before Nixon chose, any of the six outcomes could occur.

The Outcomes and Their Ranking by the Players
If the president let Cox remain, significant support for him could develop, making a later firing even more damaging.

FIGURE 2.4
PARTIAL GAME TREE OF
SATURDAY NIGHT MASSACRE GAME

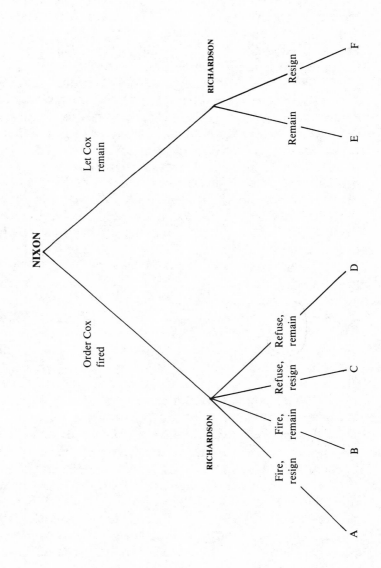

Indeed, shortly after the Cox press conference, Senators Bayh, Kennedy, Hart, and Tunney issued a joint statement saying that the "compromise" would "cripple the role" of the special prosecutor and that the president's instructions to Cox were an "unjustified challenge" to his authority.[87] This was an implicit warning that firing Cox would bring trouble.

Cox, in his press conference, stated that he would promptly seek a contempt citation against the president and even challenged the president's authority to remove him. Such open defiance, if allowed, could hamper American diplomatic efforts in the Middle East. If Richardson then remained (outcome E), there might be further attempts to negotiate with Cox or, more probably, to present the White House proposal directly to Judge Sirica, as suggested in Richardson's Saturday morning letter to the president. Given Cox's adamance and Nixon's desire for decisive action, it is likely that the president would have ultimately ordered Cox fired. If Richardson had resigned (outcome F), William Ruckelshaus would have become acting attorney general. Ruckelshaus could have attempted to continue to negotiate or resigned either immediately or in the event of a presidential firing order.

If the president ordered Richardson to fire Cox and he did so, Richardson would have violated his pledge to the Senate to remove Cox only for "extraordinary improprieties"; his reputation for honor and integrity would be shattered. Richardson would have alienated himself from his moderate Republican constituency with which he was already in trouble for his unstinting public support of Nixon policies. If Richardson remained after dismissing Cox (outcome B), the damage to his career would be irremediable. Undoubtedly, he would have been brought before the Senate Judiciary Committee where he would have faced a most hostile reception. The committee probably would have recommended, and the Congress voted, a contempt citation or a statement of censure. Again, Richardson would probably have presented the proposal to Judge Sirica (rather than request that the Court of Appeals' order be vacated).

Cox would be removed and perhaps his staff would resign en masse. The investigation and prosecution would revert to the highly tractable Justice Department, at the minimum causing a long delay and increasing the difficulty in getting guilty pleas from the prosecution targets. The president would have achieved his goals of being rid of Cox and stemming the Watergate investigation. If Richardson remained, the president's action would probably have generated less opposition than if Richardson resigned after firing Cox (outcome A). Richardson's resignation would be seen as supportive of Cox.

If Richardson refused to discharge Cox and remained attorney general (outcome D), he would have placed himself in the personally repugnant position of refusing a direct order of the president. He remained a "team player," loyal to the president.[88] He did not want to make the situation more difficult for the president. Richardson's open defiance would demonstrate that President Nixon was no longer in control of the government. The president could not let such a situation continue.

If Richardson resigned after refusing to fire Cox (outcome C), he would preserve his honor and integrity. His resignation would trigger widespread congressional and public opposition to the president (although, as we shall see, the magnitude of the response, the so-called "firestorm," surprised all the participants). Cox would no longer be isolated; the president's efforts to picture Cox as unreasonably recalcitrant would collapse. The president would be faced with the string of resignations that he wanted to avoid.

These conflicting considerations are now combined into a ranking of the six outcomes by Nixon and Richardson (and Cox). President Nixon believed that Cox's defiance gravely undermined his ability to govern. If Cox were allowed to remain special prosecutor, he would have an official forum from which to foment opposition to the president. Nixon's control of the government would be weakened. His and the nation's prestige and credibility in the world would be seriously damaged, threatening American diplomatic initiatives in the Middle East. "I thought of Brezhnev and how it would look to the Soviets if in the midst of our diplomatic showdown with them I were in the position of having to defer to the demands of one of my own employees."[89] The president clearly preferred to order Cox fired; hence (A-B-C-D,E-F).

If the president ordered Richardson to fire Cox, he surely

preferred that Richardson obey (outcome A or B); hence (A-B,C-D). If Richardson fired Cox, the president would prefer that Richardson remain attorney general (B) since the extent and intensity of opposition to the president would have been diminished; hence (B,A).

If Richardson refused to obey the order to fire Cox, the president would prefer that Richardson resign (C) than to remain (D). Richardson's resignation would have represented a disagreement over the *wisdom* of firing Cox; standing in defiance would have been a denial of the president's constitutional *authority* to dismiss Cox; hence (C,D). Finally, if the president did not order Cox fired, he would surely have preferred that Richardson remain attorney general (E) than resign (F); hence (E,F).

Putting the partial preference scales together, the president's presumed ranking of the six outcomes (from best to worst), defined by the two strategies of the president and the six of Richardson (where subscript, N, represents President Nixon and subscript, R, represents Richardson), is

B. Order Cox fired$_N$/Fire Cox, remain$_R$;
A. Order Cox fired$_N$/Fire Cox, resign$_R$;
C. Order Cox fired$_N$/Refuse, resign$_R$;
D. Order Cox fired$_N$/Refuse, remain$_R$;
E. Let Cox remain$_N$/Remain$_R$;
F. Let Cox remain$_N$/Resign$_R$.

Richardson wanted to continue negotiations with Cox or, alternatively, to bypass Cox and seek acceptance of the proposal directly from Judge Sirica. Clearly, he preferred that the president not order Cox fired if Cox defied him and remained (E or F); hence (E-F,A-B-C-D). If the president did not order Cox fired, Richardson would certainly prefer to remain (E); hence (E,F).

In the event of a presidential firing order (outcomes A,B,C,D), Richardson would prefer to refuse (C or D). Discharging the order, the attorney general would be destroying his reputation for probity and honor; he would be breaking solemn pledges to Cox and the Senate. His political dreams would be dashed. Richardson believed that Cox's position was well-founded; certainly Cox had committed no "extraordinary im-

proprieties." Dismissing Cox would destroy his efforts to re-
vitalize the Justice Department; hence (C-D,A-B).

   Richardson would prefer to resign (C) than remain (D)
after refusing to carry out the president's order. Richardson had
no desire to compound the president's problems both at home
and abroad. Richardson was questioning the president's wisdom
in this particular instance, not his general political program nor
his authority. In a press conference on October 23, Richardson
continued to emphasize his loyalty to the president: "I still believe in the general purposes of his administration."[90] Hence
(C,D).

   If Richardson were to fire Cox, he would rather resign
immediately (A) than remain (B). If he remained, his authority
as attorney general and his credibility concerning the Watergate
investigations and prosecutions would be destroyed. His political career would end with the administration. Resigning after
discharging Cox would have at least afforded Richardson the
argument that, although he disagreed with the order, he felt it
his duty to carry it out and then resign; hence (A,B).

   Putting the partial preference scales together, Richardson's presumed ranking of the six outcomes (from best to worst),
defined by the strategies of each player (where subscript, R,
represents Richardson and subscript, N, represents Nixon), is:

   E. Remain$_R$/Let Cox remain$_N$;
   F. Resign$_R$/Let Cox remain$_N$;
   C. Refuse, resign$_R$/Order Cox fired$_N$;
   D. Refuse, remain$_R$/Order Cox fired$_N$;
   A. Fire Cox, resign$_R$/Order Cox fired$_N$;
   B. Fire Cox, remain$_R$/Order Cox fired$_N$.

If the best outcome for each player is represented by "6," the
second-best by "5," and so on, the rankings of the six outcomes
in the Figure 2.4 game tree (that is, payoffs associated with these
outcomes) are shown as endpoints of the six lower branches of
the game tree in Figure 2.5.

The Analysis of the Saturday Night Massacre Game
   Richardson's and Nixon's optimal strategies and, hence,
the rational outcome of the game can be determined by exam-
ining the game tree in Figure 2.5.[91] The tree is analyzed from

FIGURE 2.5
GAME TREE OF SATURDAY NIGHT MASSACRE GAME

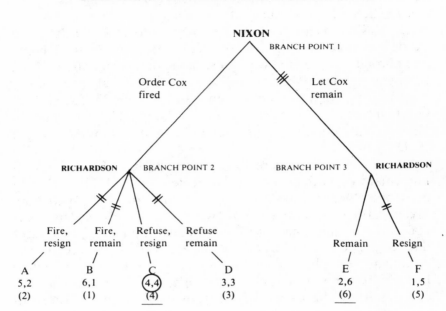

NOTE: 1. x, y = Nixon, Richardson.
2. The outcomes underlined by a solid line represent Richardson's superior outcomes at each branch point. The outcome underlined by a broken line represents Nixon's superior outcome given Richardson's subsequent optimal
choices.
3. The strategies cut by a double line are Richardson's eliminated inferior strategies. The strategy cut by a triple line is Nixon's eliminated inferior strategy.
4. The circled outcome is the rational outcome of the game.
5. The payoffs in parentheses are Cox's.

the "bottom up"; that is, one assumes Richardson, as the last-
moving player, will choose the best outcome available at each
branch point where he makes a strategy choice (branch points
2 and 3). Proceeding up the tree, the president, anticipating
Richardson's strategy choice at the two branch points and knowing his own preference scale, will choose the strategy at branch
point 1 that leads to a better outcome for himself given that
Richardson will choose the superior outcome at branch points
2 (A,B,C, or D) and 3 (E or F). At branch point 2, Richardson's

superior outcome is outcome C, providing Richardson with his third-best payoff "4". That is, if the president ordered Richardson to fire Cox, Richardson would refuse and resign. At branch point 3, Richardson's superior outcome is (E), providing Richardson with his best payoff "6". That is, if the president let Cox remain, Richardson would choose to remain.

In Figure 2.5, Richardson's preferred outcomes are underlined with a solid line. Strategies leading to inferior outcomes are eliminated, represented by a double line through these strategies.

President Nixon, realizing that Richardson's choice of strategy will lead to outcome C or E, will adopt a strategy that leads to his more preferred outcome. Since outcome C provides the president with his third-best payoff, "4," whereas outcome E provides him with his next-worst, "2," the president will choose his strategy that leads to outcome C. He will order Richardson to fire Cox.

In Figure 2.5, showing Richardson's preferred outcomes at branches 2 and 3, that which Nixon prefers is underlined with a broken line. Nixon's "let Cox remain" strategy is eliminated, as is represented by the triple line through the strategy.

Thus, successive elimination of inferior outcomes, based on Nixon's anticipation of Richardson's subsequent choices, led Nixon to order Richardson to fire Cox and Richardson to refuse and resign. Both players received their third-best payoff.

Cox preferred the president not to fire him (E or F). The special prosecutor, in his press conference, attempted to dissuade the president from firing him by declaring that only the attorney general could do so; hence (E-F,A-B-C-D). If no order to fire him was issued, Cox would prefer that Richardson remain attorney general (F), as the guarantor of his independence; hence (E,F). If Cox's threat were ineffective and the president commanded Richardson to fire Cox (outcomes A,B,C,D), Cox would naturally prefer that Richardson refuse (C or D). Although Cox would be widely supported by the public, the media, and in Congress, the fact that he was dismissed by the respected attorney general would have weakened Cox's position; hence (C-D,A-B). If Richardson refused to fire him, Cox would prefer that the attorney general resign (C). Richardson's resignation would escalate opposition to the president; hence (C,D). Finally, if Cox were fired (A or B), he would probably prefer Richardson to remain (A); hence (A,B).

Combining these partial preferences, Cox's ordering of the outcomes and their associated payoffs are (where subscript, N, represents Nixon and subscript, C, represents Cox):

E. Let Cox remain$_N$/Remain$_C$;
F. Let Cox remain$_N$/Resign$_C$;
C. Order Cox fired$_N$/Refuse, resign$_C$;
D. Order Cox fired$_N$/Refuse, remain$_C$;
A. Order Cox fired$_N$/Fire Cox, resign$_C$;
B. Order Cox fired$_N$/Fire Cox, remain$_C$.

Cox, like Nixon and Richardson, receives his third-best outcome, C, with a payoff of "4."

At 2:30 P.M., Alexander Haig called Richardson and ordered him to fire Cox. Richardson demurred and requested a meeting with the president to submit his resignation. An hour later, the president expressed extreme concern to Richardson about the Middle East situation and Brezhnev's reaction to Cox's defiance. However, Richardson felt he could neither carry out the president's order to fire Cox nor delay his resignation as the president suggested.[92] He submitted his resignation, which the president accepted.

2.6 The Game Continued: Ruckelshaus and Bork
Cox remained. After Richardson resigned, William Ruckelshaus became acting attorney general. Haig called him and ordered him to fire Cox, again citing the Middle East situation. The president's order to Ruckelshaus left him with the same choices that Richardson had. Many of the same concerns that moved Richardson to resign affected Ruckelshaus' decision. The most important consideration arose from the fact that he was chosen by Richardson to be his deputy. Ruckelshaus therefore felt bound by the same agreement that Richardson had made with the Senate regarding the special prosecutor. When asked to violate this pledge, he felt he had no choice but to refuse and then resign.[93]

With Ruckelshaus gone, Solicitor General Robert Bork became acting attorney general and was faced with the same four choices as his predecessors. Bork was not a party to the agreement with the special prosecutor and the Senate; he believed that the president had the right to order Cox fired. Bork had a basic loyalty to and sympathy for the values of the Nixon administration and a basic distrust and dislike for "liberals."[94]

Bork apparently made his decision on principle, not ambition. He was well aware of the opprobrium that would be directed against him. When he made his original decision to fire Cox, he felt that he should then resign himself. Richardson quotes him: "I don't want to stay on and be perceived as an apparatchik."[95] Both Richardson and Ruckelshaus persuaded Bork that that was not in itself a sufficient concern to justify the drastic loss of continuity at the Justice Department that would result if he also resigned.[96]

At 6:00 P.M., Bork accepted the president's order and signed a draft of a letter firing Cox.

Later that evening White House Press Secretary Ron Ziegler announced that Cox had been dismissed, Richardson had resigned, and Ruckelshaus had been discharged. He further disclosed the dissolution of the special prosecution force and the return of the Watergate investigation to the Justice Department.

At 9:00 P.M., the nation learned that the FBI had arrived at the special prosecutor's office to seal it off from its staff members, to close all files and to patrol it in force. Additionally, other FBI agents in the Department of Justice had moved to seal off the offices of the attorney general and the deputy attorney general.

2.7 The Firestorm

The reaction to the announcement of the Cox firing and the FBI occupation of the special prosecutor's and attorney general's offices was massive and overwhelmingly unfavorable to the president. Alexander Haig, drawing a military metaphor, termed it a "firestorm."

By Tuesday, October 23, Western Union had processed more than 150,000 telegrams ("the heaviest concentrated volume on record"). (At the end of ten days the total was 450,000.) Messages into congressional offices were running better than 100 to 1 against the president. An Oliver Quayle poll showed that a plurality (44 percent to 42 percent) of Americans believed that President Nixon should be impeached.[97]

Until then, impeachment had been a dreaded word, in fact, unthinkable for most in Congress and the media. Prior to the Saturday Night Massacre, there had been a great reluctance in Congress to move against the president.[98] Saturday evening, "impeachment" was cautiously voiced by several members of the Senate and House of both parties. Senator Edward Brooke, a Republican, said Nixon's act was "sufficient evidence which the House of Representatives should consider to begin impeachment proceedings."[99] Hardly any voices were raised in support of Nixon. An exception was Gerald Ford, Nixon's nominee to succeed Agnew, who said that Nixon, "had no other choice after Cox who was, after all, a subordinate, refused to accept the compromise solution to the tapes issue."[100] On Sunday, the congressional leadership began to act on impeachment.

On Monday, members of the House Democratic Party leadership met with Speaker Carl Albert to begin a study on a possible impeachment inquiry. (Even with the events of the previous three days, Congress was still afraid of impeachment. A "study" would allow them to step back.) Republican reaction continued to be unfavorable. Senator Robert Packwood of Oregon declared, "The office of President does not carry with it a license to destroy justice in America."[101] California Republican Congressman Jerry Pettis said, "I'm bending so far backwards that my fifth vertebra is about to break."[102]

Congressional Republican leaders warned the president that they could not defend him against a move toward impeachment unless he surrendered the tapes. By Wednesday, October 24, 84 members of the House of Representatives had introduced legislation (more than 20 bills) dealing with impeachment. A total of 144 representatives and 59 senators authored or cosponsored bills to create a truly independent special prosecutor.

The outrage was universal. The deans of 17 law schools petitioned Congress to "consider the necessity" of immediate impeachment. Chesterfield Smith, president of the American Bar Association, condemned Nixon for attempting to "abort the established processes of justice."[103] The AFL-CIO, meeting in Bal Harbour, Florida, called on the president to resign. The news media sharply attacked the president. Newspapers which had supported Nixon in 1972, called either for the president's impeachment or resignation.

2.8 Nixon-Sirica Game

After the events that had taken place over the weekend, Judge Sirica remained as the president's last hope of getting his proposal accepted and thus avoiding a confrontation with the courts. On Monday, October 22, White House lawyers submitted a copy of the Stennis plan and a supporting brief to Sirica. The judge called a hearing for noon the following day for the White House formally to respond to his order, as affirmed by the Court of Appeals, to surrender the subpoenaed tapes and documents.

The White House had let it be known that the president was prepared to defy a ruling by Sirica that the proposal was unacceptable. A "top White House aide" was reported to have replied, when asked what the president would do if Sirica found him in contempt, "Nothing. Congress can act if it likes."[104]

Responding to the president's threat, Sirica "fairly radiated signals" that he would reject the Stennis compromise and would cite the president for contempt.[105] On Sunday, October 21, Sirica told the president of Fairfield University that he would probably be the first federal judge in history to hold a president in contempt.[106] On Monday, he signed a protective order, requested by Cox after his removal, and summoned the two Watergate grand juries, to inform them that they were "operative and intact" and that he himself would "preserve the integrity of their proceedings."[107] His aides disclosed that he was reading up on the law of contempt.[108]

The Players and Their Strategies

When the White House lawyers appeared before Judge Sirica, they could have announced the president's choice of one of three strategies:

1. Defy the Court of Appeals order and present the "Stennis Compromise" to Judge Sirica (N_1).
2. Request an extension to file an appeal to the Supreme Court (N_2).
3. Obey the Court of Appeals order and surrender the tapes to Judge Sirica (N_3).

If the president defied the court, Judge Sirica could either

1. Accept the Stennis compromise as substantially complying with the Court of Appeals ruling (S_1).
2. Reject the Stennis compromise; cite the president for contempt (S_2).

If the president requested an extension for a Supreme Court appeal, Judge Sirica could either

1. Grant the extension (S_3).
2. Deny the extension and cite the president for contempt for not complying or appealing before the October 19 deadline (S_4).

If the president announced his intention to turn the tapes over, Judge Sirica could either

1. Accept the tapes as complying with the Court of Appeals order (S_5).
2. Reject the tapes and cite the president for contempt for not complying or appealing before the October 19 deadline (S_6).

The president's and Judge Sirica's strategies are presented in the game tree in Figure 2.6. Sirica's six strategies can be collapsed into two. Strategies S_1, S_3 and S_5 can be collapsed into:

1. Accede to President Nixon's request or actions.

Strategies S_2, S_4 and S_6 can be collapsed into:

2. Reject the president's requests or actions and cite the president for contempt.

A partial normal-form representation of the (collapsed) game between Sirica and Nixon is provided in Figure 2.7.

FIGURE 2.6
GAME TREE OF NIXON-SIRICA GAME

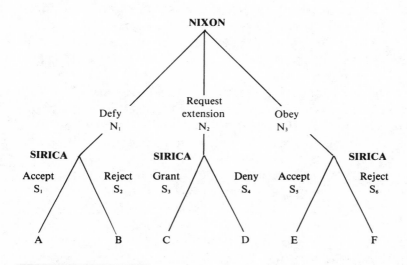

NOTE: Outcome D is unstable. After Sirica denied the request, the president would then
have the choice of defying or obeying. The outcome would have then been B or E,
respectively. This instability does not affect the subsequent analysis.

FIGURE 2.7
NORMAL-FORM OF
COLLAPSED NIXON-SIRICA GAME

SIRICA

		ACCEDE	REJECT/CITE FOR CONTEMPT
	DEFY	A. Defy/Accede	B. Defy/Cite
NIXON	REQUEST EXTENSION	C. Request/Accede	D. Request/Cite
	OBEY	E. Obey/Accede	F. Obey/Cite

The Outcomes and Their Rankings by the Players

Judge Sirica's acceptance of the Stennis compromise would stamp the proposal with a judicial imprimatur, providing an ex post facto justification for Cox's dismissal. The "firestorm" would wane and the movement to impeach would be braked. The investigation and prosecution of Watergate crimes would be severely hampered; the president and many of his men would survive Watergate.

Cox was gone. Only heavily expurgated transcripts would be released. A favorable precedent for the president in any further request for evidence would be established. The esteem and authority of the judiciary would be impaired; the president's defiance of the Court of Appeals represented a challenge to the judiciary's ability to interpret the Constitution. The courts would be perceived as having caved in to Nixon's threats.

If Judge Sirica rejected the proposal and cited the president for contempt, the integrity of the judiciary would be preserved. A contempt citation would virtually ensure impeachment, providing a "high crime" with which to charge the president. There was a good possibility of conviction. Senator Henry Jackson, no anti-Nixon radical, noted at the time that there was "no doubt in my mind" that if the president had not turned over the tapes "he would have been impeached and convicted. . . . If he violates any court order . . . he is finished."[109]

The denial of an extension, coupled with a contempt citation, would have similar effects except that Sirica's credibility might be damaged. Although such extensions were usually requested *before* the expiration of the deadline, the White House and its defenders could argue, with some plausibility, that Sirica was overzealous.[110] The focus of attention might shift to the judge's decision and away from the president's prior defiance. Likewise, if the president agreed to turn over the tapes and Sirica then cited him for contempt, the judge would be severely criticized and his position gravely weakened.

If the president were granted an extension to file a Supreme Court appeal, he would face the same risks and rewards as if he had appealed before the expiration deadline. The president's position both with the general public and in the House would continue to deteriorate. Some members of his staff believed that a request for an extension would prolong the nation's focus on the tapes and strain the president's credibility even further. After all, the president had declared on Friday evening that he was taking his action to avoid the "constitutional confrontation" that an appeal to the Supreme Court would produce. Judge Sirica would be criticized by some as having been intimidated by the president.

If the president announced his compliance and the tapes were accepted, the stature of the judiciary would be preserved, perhaps enhanced. A confrontation between the judiciary and the president would be avoided or, at least, postponed. The shock of compliance (another "big play") could regain the initiative lost in the previous five days. The White House could argue that Cox had not been fired because of damaging information on the tapes. Also, the terms of the appellate court order left White House lawyers room to fight a long delaying action to suppress portions of the tapes on national security or on other claims of confidentiality. Republican members of Congress, particularly, would be initially less reluctant to defend the president.

Compliance meant that damaging evidence would be released, evidence that established Nixon's complicity in the Watergate coverup (evidence that ultimately would lead to the adoption of impeachment Article I by the House Judiciary Committee). Also, the revelation that two tapes were "missing" and one had an eighteen and one-half minute gap would seriously erode the president's position in and out of Congress.

These conflicting considerations are now combined into a ranking of the six outcomes by the two players. Defiance would provide the president either his best or his worst outcomes. Judicial acceptance of the Stennis compromise would guarantee the achievement of Nixon's two goals to be rid of Cox and to resolve the tapes issue favorably to himself. Clearly, this would be the best he could do (outcome A). His almost certain impeachment and possible Senate conviction—the result of the commission of the "high crime" of contempt of court—represented his worst outcome (B); hence (A,C-D-E-F,B).

Being cited for contempt after announcing compliance

would represent the president's next-best outcome (F), at least in the short run, since Sirica, not he would be the center of controversy; hence (F,C-D-E).

Compliance, (E), even with its long-term risks, would be the swift action necessary to forestall "an impeachment resolution being raced through the House." Also, compliance would "reduce the temptation the Soviets would feel... to ... exploit the international crisis in the Middle East."[111] Hence, (E,C-D).

An appeal to the Supreme Court "would force an even more binding decision, possibly a negative one."[112] Impeachment would remain a real danger (C). However, the president's position in the Congress would be worse if he were cited for contempt (D); hence (C,D).

Putting these partial preference scales together, President Nixon's presumed ranking of the six outcomes (where subscript, N, represents Nixon and subscript, S, represents Sirica), was:

A. $Defy_N/Accede_S$;

F. $Obey_N/Contempt_S$;

E. $Obey_N/Accede_S$;

C. $Extend_N/Accede_S$;

D. $Extend_N/Contempt_S$;

B. $Defy_N/Contempt_S$.

Judge Sirica would manifestly prefer that President Nixon comply with the Court of Appeals order (outcome E). Compliance would avoid a constitutional crisis which would be precipitated by presidential defiance; hence (E,A-B-C-D-F).

If President Nixon defied the court (outcomes A and B), only a contempt citation (B) would preserve the institutional integrity of the judicial branch; hence (B,A). Sirica was in fundamental disagreement with the Stennis compromise for the same reasons that Cox rejected it.[113] Outcome B is Sirica's second-best; hence (E,B,A-C-D-F).

It is assumed that Sirica then preferred to accede to a presidential request for an extension to appeal to the Supreme Court (C) than to deny the request and cite the president for contempt (D). Although it may have been impolitic for the president to request the extension, refusal of the request would make Sirica's behavior, rather than the president's, the issue; hence (C,D).

Acceding to the president's defiance (A) represents Sirica's second-worst outcome. Failure to act in the face of the president's challenge to the judiciary would represent a refashioning of the Constitution—the consolidation of the "imperial presidency." Although extremely unlikely, a contempt citation following compliance (F) would be Sirica's least-desired outcome. Sirica would be widely perceived as excessively punitive, if not irrational; hence (A,F).

Putting these partial preference scales together, Judge Sirica's presumed ranking of the six outcomes (from best to worst), was

E. $Accede_S/Obey_N$;

B. $Contempt_S/Defy_N$;

C. $Accede_S/Extend_N$;

D. $Contempt_S/Extend_N$;

A. $Accede_S/Defy_N$;

F. $Contempt_S/Obey_N$.

If the best outcome for each player is represented by "6," the next-best by "5," and so on, the rankings of the six outcomes in Figure 2.7 are shown in the matrix in Figure 2.8. In this representation of the game, which assumes both players choose their strategies simultaneously (and thus independently of each other), the eventual outcome is indeterminate. There is no outcome in equilibrium. That is, at each outcome, at least one player has an incentive to change his strategy choice in expectation of a higher payoff.

However, since Sirica and Nixon did not make simultaneous choices in ignorance of each other, the payoff matrix in Figure 2.8 does not capture the dynamics of this game. President Nixon acted first; Judge Sirica chose his strategy after the president had. Figure 2.9 presents an expanded normal-form of this game.

In this representation, the president still has three stra-

FIGURE 2.8
PAYOFF MATRIX
OF NIXON-SIRICA GAME

SIRICA

		ACCEDE	REJECT/CITE FOR CONTEMPT
NIXON	DEFY	A. 6,2	B. 1,5
	REQUEST EXTENSION	C. 3,4	D. 2,3
	OBEY	E. 4,6	F. 5,1

NOTE: 1. x, y = Nixon, Sirica.
2. Neither Nixon nor Sirica have a dominant strategy; none of the outcomes are in equilibrium. There is no rational outcome.

tegies, but Judge Sirica now has eight. These eight strategies represent all the contingent strategies available to Judge Sirica given Nixon moves first. These eight strategies are:

1. Accede, regardless;

2. Contempt, regardless;

3. Contempt if defy; accede otherwise;

4. Contempt if requests; accede otherwise;

5. Contempt if obeys; accede otherwise;

6. Accede if obeys; contempt otherwise;

7. Accede if requests; contempt otherwise;

8. Accede if defy; contempt otherwise.

In this representation, citing the president for contempt if he defied and acceding otherwise (strategy 3) is a dominant strategy for Sirica: it yields payoffs as good as and, in at least one case, better than the payoffs yielded by any of his other seven strategies, whatever Nixon's strategy choice.

Given this unconditionally best strategy choice on Sirica's part, it is reasonable to assume that Nixon will anticipate its

FIGURE 2.9

EXPANDED NORMAL-FORM OF NIXON-SIRICA GAME

SIRICA

		1	2	3	4	5	6	7	8
	DEFY	6,2	1,5	1,5	6,2	6,2	1,5	1,5	6,2
NIXON	REQUEST EXTENSION	3,4	2,3	3,4	2,3	3,4	2,3	3,4	2,3
	OBEY	4,6	5,1	(4,6)	4,6	5,1	4,6	5,1	5,1

Sirica has a dominant strategy.

Nixon "obeys" in anticipation of Sirica's choice.

NOTE: 1. x, y, = Nixon, Sirica.

2. A specification of Sirica's eight strategies can be found on p. 104.

3. The circled outcome (4,6) is in equilibrium; Sirica's "cite if defiance, accede otherwise" strategy is dominant.

choice. To maximize his payoff, the president will choose the strategy which yields the highest payoff in the column associated with Sirica's dominant strategy (the third column in Figure 2.9) Since "4" is better than "3" or "1", we would expect that Nixon would choose the "obey" strategy. Sirica gets his best outcome; Nixon his third best.

In fact, on Tuesday afternoon, October 23, Charles Alan Wright announced to a shocked courtroom that the president would fully comply with the Court of Appeals order: "This President does not defy the law."[114] (Judge Sirica has since spelled out his intended course of action if the president defied.

> [S]omeone who defied court orders as Nixon had would be inviting . . . a stretch in jail for contempt. I knew I couldn't order the president arrested, although I must admit the thought occurred to me more than once that weekend.[115]

Instead, Sirica would have found the president in contempt and then "would levy a stiff fine to try to force compliance."

> I knew the president loved money. . . . I decided to hit him in his pocketbook; I would fine him between $35,000 and $50,000 for each day the tapes weren't turned over.[116]

Sirica was certain that Nixon would have complied quickly. He was equally certain that the Court of Appeals would have upheld the fines since it supported the subpoena in the first place).[117]

2.9 Information and Rationality

Given the public and congressional reaction to Cox's firing and Richardson's and Ruckelshaus' resignations, "the president was widely thought to have acted rashly and foolishly, in a fit of pique at best and of irrational frustration and anger at worst."[118] Some observers believed that Nixon had gone insane. Carl Rowan asked, "Has President Nixon gone crazy?"; Ralph Nader declared that Nixon was "acting like a madman."[119]

The appearance of irrationality arose since only one of the major consequences of the president's actions, the removal of Special Prosecutor Cox and the transfer of his staff and functions to the Justice Department, was foreseen and intended. Among the unforeseen and unintended consequences were the resignations of Richardson and Ruckelshaus and the instant and enormous increase in public and congressional demands for resignation or impeachment of the president and his surrender of the tapes to Judge Sirica.

As the game-theoretic analysis demonstrates, given the information and choices available to him, the president acted rationally. (In game-theoretic terms, *information* determines the extent to which a player can take into account the possible actions of the other players. The *communication* of this information determines the extent to which players can coordiante their strategies.) A major error that the president made in the Saturday Night Massacre "game" was in not foreseeing Richardson's resignation. However, when he acted on Friday and Saturday, the president and his aides felt that Richardson would "squirm" but ultimately acquiesce to Cox's firing. As we have seen, this was a reasonable inference from Richardson's past behavior. Richardson introduced uncertainty and confusion into the game by failing to make his preferences clear.

An element of irrationality, however, lies in the president's reliance on intermediaries to deal with Richardson. Given the tremendous potential costs involved in his actions, the president failed to determine directly Richardson's preferences. There was no meeting between the president and Richardson, nor even a telephone conversation during the entire week preceding the Saturday Night Massacre. Until Richardson actually tendered his resignation on Saturday afternoon, Nixon did not know what Richardson would do.[120] Richardson, in a press conference on October 23, when asked if the president had reason to expect him to resign, stated, "The question of what I would do, I think, was unclear from his perspective up to the point on Saturday afternoon when I came to see him."[121]

Also, given the information available to him, the president's action toward Cox was reasonable. It was the belief, shared by the president, his lawyers, his closest advisors and Richardson that Cox would resign in protest when faced with the prohibition on access. If Cox had indeed resigned, the game would have ended far differently, far more favorably both to the president and Richardson. However, the White House seriously misread both the strategies available to Cox and Cox's evaluation

and ranking of the outcomes. Also, it is difficult to see how the
White House could believe that Cox would reject the proposal,
remain and *do nothing* in the face of his adamance on the need
for the tapes as the best available evidence.

Furthermore, the "firestorm' completely surprised the
players. According to Richardson:

> . . . although I could have foreseen that the firing and the two
> resignations would in combination produce a considerable public
> uproar, I could not have guessed that, all across the country,
> many others felt as strongly about the day's events.[122]

And Nixon:

> Although I had been prepared for a major and adverse reaction
> to Cox's firing, I was taken by surprise by the ferocious intensity
> that actually occurred. . . . To the extent that I had not been
> aware of this situation [the depth of Watergate's impact], my
> actions were the result of a serious miscalculation.[123]

Finally, Nixon's capitulation on Tuesday was a rational
response to the changed strategic environment. From Friday
evening to Tuesday afternoon, the president's evaluation of the
outcomes—in fact, the very nature of the outcomes—changed
radically. Clearly, the president on Friday and Saturday believed
in the efficacy of the Stennis compromise, preferring to impose
it rather than comply or appeal to the Supreme Court. Even as
late as Sunday, October 21, the White House assessment was
that Congress had neither the evidence nor the will to move
against the president. This evaluation had so changed by Tuesday that impeachment seemed imminent. By Tuesday, the
"rules" of the game had changed, that is, there was a significant
change in the decisional environment. Public, and more important, congressional outrage had made defiance tantamount to
impeachment. Henceforth, impeachment became the key strategic variable; avoiding impeachment became the president's all-
consuming goal.

The president's extreme fear of and antipathy to Cox and
his "liberal enclave" could be considered, in a popular sense,
to be "irrational." However, given this antipathy, Nixon acted
rationally in respect to it. He fired Cox. Goals and "feelings"
are neither rational or irrational; only strategy choices are.[124]

2.10 Could It Have Ended Differently?

Since the "firestorm" and the resulting devastation to the president's position resulted from Cox's public rejection of the White House proposal and the subsequent resignations of Richardson and Ruckelshaus, the question must be raised: What actions might the president have chosen to produce outcomes far more favorable to him?

A key element in the historical game appears to be that the president prohibited Cox from subpoenaing additional evidence. The president's major miscalculation was in believing that the prohibition on access would solidify Cox's (presumed) inclination to resign. In fact, by asserting that the special prosecutor could not subpoena additional evidence, the president was playing into Cox's hand by providing a justification for his defiance. Rather than having the White House and *Richardson* against Cox, the president was forcing Richardson to side with the special prosecutor. There is evidence that as late as Thursday evening the idea of putting forward the proposal without the prohibition on access was still being considered.[125]

It was the prohibition on access, not the rest of the proposal, on which Richardson based his resignation.[126] If there were no prohibition on access, it appears that Richardson would have definitely stayed, as would Ruckelshaus. There would have been no Saturday Night Massacre. The firing order may never have been necessary since Cox, realizing that Richardson would not resign and that he would be viewed as the "wrecker of a reasonable compromise", would not have publicly confronted the president. (Clearly, the "compromise" could be more reasonably argued to be in the spirit of the Court of Appeals ruling.) If Cox still held the press conference, would he have received anywhere near the public support that he actually did? Without the prohibition on access, it is reasonable to assume that Senators Ervin and Baker would not have backed off from the agreement. Moreover, there may not have been any outcry from any of the other members of the Ervin committee. Perhaps Cox, feeling himself isolated, would have resigned. Although less likely, Richardson might have persuaded Cox to accept the "compromise" as presented or in a form that would have met the president's goals. The inclusion of the prohibition on access surely led to the fulfillment of Nixon's prime goal: to be rid of Cox. But it was done at the expense of resolving the tapes issue in his favor.

Another significant "might have been" concerns Richardson's response to Nixon's firing order. If Richardson had refused to fire Cox but had not resigned, the events on Saturday could have been very different. Would President Nixon have then fired Richardson and thereafter Ruckelshaus? Might not the "firestorm" have seemed more likely and thereby at least delayed the president's action? In any event, if Bork had not acceded and been fired or resigned himself, there would have been no way to remove Cox. The law did not provide for any further succession in the Justice Department. It is almost certain that the Senate would never have confirmed another attorney general without the assurance that Cox would remain.[127]

2.11 Expansion of the Conflict
None of the players foresaw the devastating impact of Cox's press conference on the outcome of the game, although Cox surely intended the press conference to escalate opposition to the president.

The Saturday Night Massacre game provides a vivid illustration of E. E. Schattschneider's concept of the "contagiousness of conflict."[128] Schattschneider contends that the outcome of every conflict is determined by "the extent that the audience becomes involved." Conflicts are won or lost by the success the combatants have in getting the audience involved in the fight, or excluding it, as the case may be. The widening involvement of the audience so changes the nature of the conflict (due to the unequal reinforcement of each side) that the original participants are apt to lose control of the conflict altogether.

Schattschneider notes that the scope of a conflict can be most easily restricted at the very beginning. This is because, in extremely small conflicts, the relative strengths of the contestants are known in advance. The stronger side may impose its will on the weaker without an overt test of strength because people are not apt to fight if they are sure to lose.

In the Saturday Night Massacre game, President Nixon

had attempted to isolate Cox in order to limit severely the scope of the conflict. Richardson's support, or at least acquiescence, and the participation of Stennis, an influential member of the Senate, and Ervin and Baker as the ranking members of the Senate Watergate Committee, would have ensured this isolation.

The White House directive of Friday evening is an excellent example of an audience-excluding strategy. The issue was portrayed as the president against Cox, the nation's highest elected official against a disaffected and unreasonable employee. The balance of forces weighed heavily against Cox. Thus, the hope and expectation at the White House was that Cox would resign rather than continue the struggle. However, Cox's Saturday afternoon press conference radically altered the configuration of power. "Cox's press conference was . . . a turning point in the controversy, and made a foregone conclusion of the nationwide reaction of fury at Nixon . . . ."[129] The press conference expanded the participants in the conflict by tens of millions. Theodore White notes that "the Special Prosecutor opened at his best and proceeded to get better."[130] Cox's performance has been characterized as "disarming and devastating,"[131] and "consummate television."[132]

Immediately after Ronald Zeigler's announcement of the Cox firing, the news media dramatically increased audience involvement. Regular programming was interrupted and national news correspondents, breathless and shaken, reported on the president's action. NBC and CBS presented 90-minute news specials that "spread consternation nationwide."[133] And, finally, news reports were issued that the FBI, at the president's order, occupied and sealed off the special prosecutor's offices as well as the offices of Richardson and Ruckelshaus. According to Mankiewicz

> It was unthinkable that the mild mannered, impeccably correct, law abiding man that they [the American people] had seen on television that day required the presence of the F.B.I. in his office, to prevent—what?[134]

The audience involvement grew until, on Tuesday, October 23, the president capitulated, a victim of the most effective of political strategies—the expansion of the scope of conflict.

2.12 Richardson and Cox: Saints? Strategists?

Elliot Richardson and Archibald Cox became folk heroes following the Saturday Night Massacre. Richardson's political
stock increased greatly; he began to be mentioned as a possible
Republican candidate in the 1976 presidential election. His reputation for probity and rectitude was firmly established. His
image as a man of principle and conscience was not confined to
the public at large but was accepted by scholars as well. Richardson is one of the central figures of Professors Weisband
and Franck's well-regarded *Resignation in Protest*, a study of
the behavior of high government officials who chose to resign
their positions in dispute over prevailing administration policy.[135]

Weisband and Franck argue that the essential political
and ethical choice that disagreeing officials have is between
"loyalty to team" and "loyalty to conscience" in American
public life.[136] The authors found that only ten such officials have
made their disagreements public, that the "more acceptable,
expected, behavior is a return briefly to private life, offending
no one, keeping the public in the dark on the nature of the
dispute—and making oneself available to return to the fold."[137]

Richardson is a central figure in Weisband and Franck's
second chapter, "Fighting Back and Going Public." According
to them, "Richardson found it . . . inconceivable that he should
stay on, or leave without a public utterance when the ethical and
constitutional issues were so great."[138] Richardson's behavior
was a "significant victory of ethical autonomy over expediency
and groupthink."[139]

As we have seen, Richardson's "canonization" is unjustified. Richardson did his best to persuade Cox of the desirability
of the White House proposal, a proposal which would have
deprived the special prosecutor of the best available evidence
of criminal conduct. Its adoption would have given the president
an effective means of emasculating the Watergate prosecution.

Richardson, on Saturday morning, in a final effort to save
his job, formally proposed that Cox be bypassed, that "an effort
be made to persuade Judge Sirica to accept" the proposal. Furthermore, he suggested that

> . . . in any future situation where Mr. Cox seeks judicial process
> to obtain the record of Presidential conversations would be ap-

proached on the basis of the precedent established with prespect to the Watergate tapes.[140]

Richardson's resignation can be seen not to have been made on principle but rather on expediency. Cox's press conference put Richardson in an untenable position. Remaining would have destroyed his reputation. Also, the nature of the situation precluded him from taking the usual resignation route examined by Weisband and Franck. The policy at issue was not confined to the privacy of government councils; it was dramatized before millions. He could not have resigned citing "personal," "family" or "financial" reasons. He had no choice but publicly to address the issues in some way. But even in his resignation letter Richardson did his utmost not to antagonize the president. After citing his commitments to the special prosecutor and the Senate, Richardson continued: "While I fully respect the reasons that have led you to conclude that the Special Prosecutor must be discharged . . . I feel I have no choice but to resign. . . ."[141] After expressing his "lasting gratitude" to the president, Richardson concluded

> It has been a privilege to share in your efforts to make the structure of world peace more stable and the structure of our own government more responsive. I believe profoundly in the rightness and importance of these efforts. . . .[142]

The following Tuesday, Richardson was defending the president and sidestepping the constitutional issues. In a news conference, Richardson defended the president's bypassing the normal procedure of appealing to the Supreme Court.

> Had he insisted on exercising that right [appeal], however, the issue would have been the subject of continuing litigation controversy for a prolonged additional period. . . .[143]

(This was the same rationale that the White House gave in its Friday night directive.) He declined to take a position on the legality of the White House proposal, stating that it was for "a judge to decide." When asked if he felt that the president was trying to limit the Cox investigation through him, he responded that he did not.[144]

According to close associates, Richardson's "greatest regret, overriding the issues in dispute, was that circumstances had forced him to the sidelines."[145] Richardson's mild responses to the president can be explained, if as reported, he believed that he would be offered another post in the Nixon administration.[146]

Theodore White has described Archibald Cox as "a man of inflexible New England rectitude," which appears to be accurate.[147] During his 30-year career in and out of government, Cox showed himself "tenacious on matters of principle and questions that he believed infringed on the majesty of law."[148] It appears that Cox saw the tapes case as resting on a clear principle—his right to obtain the material he needed for the thorough investigation and prosecution of Watergate crimes. However, Cox was far more than a man of principle; he was also a skillful strategist. His performance at his press conference was masterful. He successfully broke out of the isolation that the president had carefully constructed. He neutralized Ervin and Baker's acceptance of the proposal. Most significantly, he forced Richardson to make the decision to support his actions, a decision, as we have seen, Richardson was reluctant to make.

3

When the Court . . . ruled 8–0 against Nixon, it unknowingly
averted what might have been a supremely critical
confrontation between the Executive and Judiciary . . .
H. R. Haldeman, *The Ends of Power*

The problem was not just that we had lost but that we lost so
decisively. We had counted on some air in the Court's ruling.
We had counted on at least one dissent.
Richard Nixon, *RN*

The White House
Tapes Game

3.1 Jaworski's Appointment to the Mitchell et al. Indictments
President Nixon's capitulation on the tapes issue failed to stem
the public and congressional outrage over the Saturday Night
Massacre. Legislation was introduced in both the House and the
Senate to empower the courts to appoint a new special prosecutor entirely independent of the White House.[1] To forestall
congressional action, President Nixon, on October 26, rescinded
his weeklong "abolition" of the special prosecutor's office; he
announced that Acting Attorney General Bork would soon name
a special prosecutor who would have "independence" and the
"total cooperation" of the White House. Significantly, however,
this cooperation would not include turning over any further tapes
and documents relating to "presidential conversations."[2]

    The man the White House was wooing for the job was
Leon Jaworski, an "establishment man," a corporate lawyer;
a director of three banks and four corporations; a former president of the American Bar Association; and a conservative Texas
Democrat.[3] Jaworski apparently seemed to the president to be
"the docile special prosecutor he had been looking for from the
start."[4] This assessment was shared by those fearing a whitewash. Richard Ben-Veniste and George Frampton, both members of the special prosecutor's Watergate task force, describe
the feelings of Cox's staff toward Jaworski: "To us, Jaworski
represented the man President Nixon had procured to perpetrate
the biggest fix of all time."[5]

    Jaworski, however, was resisting White House blandish-
ments. He wanted formal safeguards guaranteeing his independence lest he meet the same end as Cox. (Indeed, Jaworski had
been offered the job by Richardson the previous May but turned
it down because he did not believe that the position had sufficient

independence.) Furthermore, he demanded that he be empowered to seek evidence in the courts. On October 31, the White House agreed that Jaworski could not be fired without the "substantial concurrence" of eight men—the majority and minority leaders of the Senate, the Speaker and minority leader of the House, and the chairman and ranking Republican of both the Senate and House Judiciary Committees.[6] He was also given the power to sue the president for evidentiary material. Jaworski then agreed to take the job.

The president had given up much, but he wanted Jaworski very badly. On that day, Fred Buzhardt informed Judge Sirica that two of the nine recordings that the president had been ordered to turn over did not exist. Buzhardt claimed that one conversation, on June 20, 1972 between Nixon and John Mitchell, his campaign manager, had been conducted on a telephone that was not connected to the White House taping system. The other, an April 15, 1973 conversation between Nixon and Dean, had not been recorded due to a malfunctioning machine.

The following day, November 1, the president announced the nomination of Senator William Saxbe of Ohio to be the new attorney general. Acting Attorney General Bork announced Jaworski's appointment and described the guarantees to which the president had agreed. (On November 5, in testimony before the House Judiciary Committee, Bork made it clear that he would resign if the White House interfered with the new special prosecutor's investigation.)[7]

The appointment of a new special prosecutor did little to dampen the outrage that the revelation of the "missing" tapes triggered. Democratic Senators Inouye and Tunney immediately called for Nixon's resignation. The president's former friends and supporters quickly joined the assault. Senator Brooke, who actively campaigned for Nixon in 1968 and 1972, stated that the president had lost the country's confidence and, therefore, "in the interests of the nation . . . he should step down, should tender his resignation." Barry Goldwater urged the president to appear before the Ervin committee to answer questions regarding the tapes. Senate Minority Leader Scott called on the president to "give the people all the information and let them judge."[8]

Media reaction was overwhelmingly unfavorable. The *New York Times, The Denver Post*, and the *Detroit News* called for Nixon's immediate resignation. The *Washington Post* proposed "exorcising" the president through impeachment, trial, and conviction.[9] *Time* issued the first editorial in its fifty-year history, "The President Should Resign":

> Richard Nixon . . . has irredeemably lost his moral authority, the confidence of most of the country, and therefore his ability to govern effectively. The nightmare of uncertainty must be ended.[10]

The president's position deteriorated further on November 21, when it was revealed that there was an 18½ minute gap in the middle of a taped conversation between Nixon and Haldeman on June 20, 1972, just three days after the Watergate break-in. Tortured White House explanations—from the influence of a "sinister force"[11] to presidential secretary Rosemary Woods' gymnastic gyrations—made matters worse.

In the second week in November, President Nixon began a drive to regain the Watergate initiative after the Saturday Night Massacre and the tapes revelations (dubbed by the press "Operation Candor"). To restore his credibility he took his case to Congress, to the Republican party, and to the American public. He met with Republican congressional leaders on November 9. Starting November 13 and continuing the rest of the week he met with all 234 Republican members of Congress as well as a group of moderate and conservative Democrats. From November 15 to 20, he took his case to the "nation." On November 15 he addressed 4000 members of the National Association of Realtors. The following day he began a five-day swing through the South, the only region where he retained a measure of his former popularity. His first stop was Disney World; his second, Macon, Georgia. His final stop was Memphis, Tennessee, where he addressed the Republican Governor's Conference.

Also at this time, the president embarked on a "honeymoon" with investigators. He promised "full cooperation" and handed over to the special prosecutor material on the milk and ITT cases and publicly released records of his personal finances.[12]

The president's public-relations offensive had some positive effect on his public standing; he gained several points in both the Harris and Gallup polls, the first such rise in several months. (Gallup showed an "approval" rate of 31 percent for the period from November 30 to December 3 compared to 27 percent for November 2 to 5; Harris showed that 37 percent of the respondents rated Nixon's performance as "good" or "excellent" in November compared to 32 percent in October.)[13]

The "honeymoon" with the special prosecutor did not last long, however. In mid-December, Jaworski began meeting with Buzhardt and Haig to discuss access to Watergate material; Nixon told Haig to give "nothing more" to Jaworski.[14] According to Attorney General Saxbe, the president's aides repeatedly requested him to intervene with Jaworski to "stop this type of activity, this infringement of executive privilege."[15]

Thus, by the end of December the president reversed course once again. He abandoned his effort to fight the case in public and "reverted to a tight-fisted, close-to-the-chest stance with heavy emphasis on a tenacious legal defense."[16] This tactical shift was signalled on January 4 by the retaining of James St. Clair, a noted Boston trial lawyer, to replace Buzhardt as the president's chief Watergate lawyer.

On January 9, Jaworski requested twenty-five tapes that he believed related to the Watergate cover-up. He repeated his request at a meeting with St. Clair on January 22. St. Clair stalled; he told Jaworski that a decision would be made shortly.

The president's strategy appeared to the special prosecutor's staff to be "endless foot-dragging without any concrete refusal to provide evidence."[17] The specter of impeachment was haunting the president.[18] He must have been worried that the special prosecutor would turn over material to the House Judiciary Committee. However, he could not simply deny Jaworski's request; a flat refusal would give Jaworski grounds for notifying Congress that the president had ceased cooperating. Since Jaworski had recently reported to Congress that the White House was cooperating, a contrary report would damage the president's impeachment defense.

Jaworski attempted to allay the president's fears that he would turn over presidential tapes and documents to the Congress. On January 12 he publicly stated that he could "see no way at the present time" to make any materials gathered in the Watergate investigation available to the House Judiciary Committee.[19]

On January 30, Jaworski pressed the White House for a decision on all outstanding requests for presidential evidence. That evening President Nixon delivered his State of the Union address. He declared that he had given the special prosecutor "all the material that he needs to conclude his investigation and to proceed to prosecute the guilty and to clear the innocent." He called for the speedy end to all the Watergate probes, "One year of Watergate is enough."[20] The next day St. Clair indicated that no more tapes and documents would be forthcoming; he told Jaworski that he hoped the president could continue to cooperate but that "there has to come an end at some point."[21]

Jaworski publicly responded on February 3. In a television interview, he revealed the president's intransigence and threatened to subpoena the materials that the president refused to turn over. That afternoon St. Clair informed Jaworski that Nixon had rejected all outstanding requests for tapes and documents.

Thus, by early February, three months after his appointment, Jaworski "found himself facing just what Archibald Cox had confronted the fall before: a White House stonewall."[22] Jaworski turned to the Congress for support. On February 14, he wrote to Senate Judiciary Committee Chairman James Eastland reporting the president's refusal to submit any more tapes and documents, specifically, 27 recordings of meetings between Nixon and his aides relating to the Watergate break-in and coverup and six tapes relating to contributions made in 1972 by the dairy industry, activities of the "Plumbers," and the ITT case. (Jaworski conspicuously noted that the president had not based his refusal on claims that the particular tapes were unrelated to the prosecutor's investigations.) Jaworski told Eastland that he had assured St. Clair that if the requested material were turned over, he would make no further requests. Nonetheless, Jaworski reported that the president "refused to reconsider his earlier decision to terminate his cooperation."[23] Jaworski was warning the president, as had Cox, that he was not facing the president alone, that he was also dealing with the Senate, a body that might ultimately be called upon to judge the president's fitness for office.

3.2 Indictments to Supreme Court Oral Arguments

On March 1, 1974 the Watergate grand jury indicted seven former White House and Nixon campaign aides: John Mitchell, H. R. Haldeman, John Ehrlichman, Charles Colson, Robert Mardian, Kenneth Parkinson, and Gordon Strachan. The indictment charged that the seven men and others "known and unknown" conspired to "obstruct justice . . . to make false statements to the FBI and the grand jury . . . to defraud the United States." The defendants "by deceit, craft and trickery" subverted the CIA; destroyed records; "covertly" raised cash and paid it to the original seven Watergate defendants; offered "leniency, executive clemency" to Hunt, Liddy, McCord and Magruder; and attempted to obtain financial assistance from the CIA for the original defendants.[24]

Although the indictment was expected, it came as a "hammer blow."[25] According to Ben-Veniste and Frampton:

> . . . the impact of the indictment on the public appeared to be greater than some of the unanticipated disclosures of the past few months—the missing tapes, the eighteen-minute gap, the cloud on the President's taxes. Obviously indictment of so many of the President's intimate associates was the kind of thing public opinion did not 'discount' in advance.

> Perhaps the stamp of legal formality placed on these charges— even charges that had been circulating in the public arena for months—had greater currency with the American people than anyone expected.[26]

However, it was the grand jury's secret report and an accompanying briefcase of evidence relating to the president's role in the scandal that piqued the public's curiosity and spurred intense speculation. The grand jury informed Judge Sirica that it desired the material to be turned over to the House Judiciary· Committee.

During January and February, the prosecutors debated what action, if any, should be taken against the president. Essentially, they saw themselves as having three choices. They could

Indict Richard Nixon; decline to indict him because of Constitutional doubts or simple discretion, but list him as one of the unindicted conspirators in the Watergate cover-up case; do neither, and turn over all the evidence pertaining to Nixon's alleged criminal activity to the House impeachment committee.[27]

Members of the special prosecutor's Watergate Task Force had concluded that the president could be prosecuted for

. . . obstruction of justice, for bribery, for obstruction of a criminal investigation, and for conspiracy to commit all these offenses. In addition, he could conceivably be charged for having aided, abetted, and counseled the payment of a bribe, for having failed to report what he knew about the cover-up as an accessory after the fact, and for misprision of a felony.[28]

They vigorously argued for an indictment, that the strongest case at trial against the president's aides would be one that presented the entire coverup story to the jury, including the president's role.[29]

Jaworski disagreed. If Richard Nixon were indicted, "there would be all hell to pay." There would be a Supreme Court battle at the wrong time on the wrong question. In the end the prosecutors would lose. Nixon would not resign and the results of the abstract legal battle over the question of whether a sitting president could be indicted would bolster the president's position in the House.[30] Jaworski did not want to "get out ahead of public opinion," to appear to be "challenging" the president based on evidence not yet made public. To do so could be "fatal" to all the special prosecutor's efforts since the propriety of his actions, rather than the evidence against the president, would become the central public issue.[31] Simply, Jaworski feared that indicting Nixon would endanger the prosecution of his associates.

Ultimately, the prosecutors decided to name Nixon as an unindicted conspirator but not to publicly release his status and to submit the evidence and a "road map," which established

Nixon's criminal involvement, to Judge Sirica with a grand jury recommendation that they be turned over to the House Judiciary Committee.[32]

The efficacy of the special prosecutor's strategy became apparent on March 6, when Judge Sirica held a hearing on the grand jury proposal. The president could not publicly oppose the transfer of evidence; to do so would look as if he were simply trying to protect himself. It would have been too obvious a continuation of the coverup. Nixon had been maintaining for weeks that the House Judiciary Committee was the appropriate forum to determine his fate. He had repeatedly promised his "full cooperation" with the impeachment inquiry. However, John Wilson, H. R. Haldeman's attorney, led the attack for the president, arguing that release of the materials to the committee would generate publicity prejudicial to his client's trial. On March 18, Judge Sirica ruled that the materials would be turned over to the committee, noting that "the person on whom the report focuses, the President of the United States, has not objected to its release to the Committee."[33]

On March 12, Jaworski wrote to St. Clair requesting access to 64 taped conversations. He received no reply. On April 11 he repeated his request but this time warned that if the president continued to deny the materials to the prosecutors he would be "compelled by my responsibilities to seek appropriate judicial process."[34] The tapes issue would be in the courts again for the first time since Cox's firing.

Five days later, having received no response, Jaworski requested Judge Sirica to issue a subpoena ordering the president to furnish the tapes and records of 64 presidential conversations with Dean, Colson, Haldeman, and Ehrlichman that took place between June 1972 and June 1973. Jaworski argued that the information contained in the records was necessary for both the prosecutors and the defendants to construct their cases. Two of the defendants, Charles Colson and Robert Mardian, joined Jaworski's request. The White House refused comment. Sirica issued the subpoena on April 18 and set a May 2 deadline for the president to respond. (Meanwhile, on April 11, the House Judiciary Committee subpoenaed 42 tapes.)

Thus, by the third week in April, Nixon was caught in a

". . . pincer movement: the criminal process crowding him on one flank and political pressures overtaking him on the other."[35] There were escalating demands for material from the House and the special prosecutor. The president and his aides assumed that the contents of the tapes, particularly the damning March 21 tape, would be leaked—and leaked in the most harmful way to the president by the House committee.[36] Therefore, the president decided to release heavily edited verbatim transcripts of 46 taped conversations.

The release of the transcripts was another of Nixon's "big plays." It would demonstrate his "full cooperation." He would be "the frankest President in history, washing all his dirty linen in public, holding nothing back."[37] Nixon apparently convinced himself that the tapes (except for the ones recorded on March 21) would not hurt him much. (On June 4, 1973, after reviewing several tapes, Nixon inquired of Zeigler, "Really, the goddam record is not bad, is it?")[38]

On April 29, one year less a day after he announced the "resignations" of Haldeman, Dean and Ehrlichman, President Nixon went before the American people in a "masterfully orchestrated show"[39] and announced the release of the taped transcripts. The president also released a 50 page "summary" of the transcripts designed to place the conversations in the most favorable light.

The public reaction to this latest "big play," like that to the Saturday Night Massacre, was devastating to the president. The president's friends, apparently feeling betrayed, were among the most critical. Columnist Joseph Alsop called the transcripts "sheer flesh-crawling repulsion." William Randolph Hearst called Nixon "a man totally absorbed in the sleaziest kind of conniving." Billy Graham "deplored" the moral tone. Most ominously for the president's prospects in Congress, Senate Minority Leader Hugh Scott, a faithful Nixon apologist, called the transcripts "deplorable, disgusting, shabby and immoral."[40]

Having dealt with the House Judiciary Committee, St. Clair announced in Judge Sirica's courtroom on May 1 that the president refused to submit the subpoenaed materials to the special prosecutor. St. Clair sought an order quashing the subpoena. He argued that the subpoenaed tapes could not be used as evidence because they were "inadmissable hearsay."

St. Clair and Nixon had evidently concluded that the prosecutors, by failing to name the president as an unindicted conspirator, had committed a serious blunder: If the president's taped conversations were not part of the charged conspiracy, then they could not be admissable evidence. St. Clair also argued that the special prosecutor, as a member of the executive branch and a subordinate of the president, could not sue his superior, that is, the special prosecutor lacked "standing" to sue. (This was the same argument that former presidential legal advisor Charles Alan Wright had tried unsuccessfully to use against Cox.)

But the "standing" argument was specious. When Jaworski was appointed he was given the legal power to contest in court his quest for evidence; the president had formally ceded power of control over his "employee."

Four days later, the special prosecutor tried his own "big play." At a meeting with Haig and St. Clair, Jaworski revealed that the grand jury had named the president as a conspirator, and threatened to reveal the grand jury's action to convince Judge Sirica that the subpoenaed tapes were indeed "evidentiary."

The president and his lawyer had miscalculated. Ben-Veniste and Frampton reasonably content that the miscalculation was

> . . . undoubtedly based on our ability to keep the monumental fact of the grand jury's action secret for so long. The White House, attributing their own values to us, must have believed that if the grand jury had taken any action against the President we would have leaked it by now.[41]

Jaworski offered Nixon a deal that would spare the president the embarassment of revealing the grand jury's action: The prosecutors would drop the subpoena if the president would turn over 38 of the 64 tapes. St. Clair requested a week delay and Sirica granted it.

The president was thus faced with two choices. He could give Jaworski the tapes with their damaging revelations or delay delivery until the Supreme Court ordered it (assuming that the court ruled against him) but suffering, meanwhile, the public knowledge that the grand jury was convinced that Nixon was an integral part of a conspiracy to obstruct justice.

Unknown to the special prosecutor, Nixon on May 6 and 7 listened to 16 of the 64 subpoenaed tapes. On the afternoon of May 7 St. Clair advised Jaworski and Judge Sirica that the president would not yield the tapes. Nixon's refusal confirmed to Jaworski

> . . . that there was information in [the tapes] somewhere that would completely destroy his position or bring further harm to Haldeman or Ehrlichman. He was willing to be named publicly as an unindicted co-conspirator rather than let that information be revealed.[42]

After hearing arguments, Judge Sirica upheld the subpoena order on May 20. That day, Jaworski sent another letter to Senator Eastland charging the president with making a "farce" of the special prosecutor's office and "undercutting" his role as an independent investigator by challenging his right to sue for evidence.[43] The next day the committee voted 14–1 for a resolution supporting the special prosecutor (Senator Kennedy voted against it saying it did not go far enough in supporting Jaworski). Although it had no legal force, the resolution was a political and public relations blow to the president. The Senators feared that the president was considering firing Jaworski (as he had Cox in similar circumstances), and they felt that the resolution might deter him.[44]

As expected, on May 24, St. Clair filed an appeal in the Court of Appeals which, it seemed, would result in the postponement of the coverup trial. The reason for the probable delay was that the Court of Appeals, even if it accelerated its procedures, would not decide the case for months. If he lost, Nixon was certain to appeal to the Supreme Court, which normally recesses from June until the beginning of October. The trial of *Mitchell et al.*, scheduled for September 9, would have to be delayed until all matters related to impeachment—hearings by the House Judiciary Committee, House floor debate, and, possibly, a Senate trial—had been settled. Even if Jaworski won in the Supreme Court and got the tapes, it would take weeks to screen and transcribe them. The prosecutors worried that the witnesses in the coverup trial were already "growing stale."[45] Also, if there were a delay, James Neal, the brilliant Tennessee trial lawyer, would not be available to prosecute the case.

This delay was crucial for the president. If he were to release the newly subpoenaed materials to the special prosecutor, they would probably be made available to the House Judiciary Committee and would severely damage his impeachment defense. To Clark Mollenhoff, a pre-Watergate presidential aide turned "enemy," the president's strategy was obvious:

> He stressed constantly that the courts were the proper forum for deciding the guilt or innocence of the parties and the proper limits of executive privilege. As the lower court decisions went against him he bent just enough to seem to comply while avoiding the appeal which would have established the "definitive decision" that he claimed to want.[46]

The special prosecutor moved quickly to prevent any further delay. On the same day as the appeal by St. Clair was filed in the Court of Appeals, the prosecutors, using a seldom-invoked procedure went to the Supreme Court and sought a writ of *certiorari before judgment* that would leapfrog the appellate court. Citing the imminent coverup trial date, Jaworski noted the necessity to settle expeditiously an issue that was paralyzing the government. He requested the court not only to issue the writ but also, because the "imperative public importance" of the case required "immediate settlement," to stay in session into the summer. This way the case could be decided in sufficient time that the tapes could be used as evidence at the trial should Judge Sirica's ruling be upheld.

This strategem posed serious risks for the special prosecutor. Only twice since World War II had the Supreme Court taken a case under the "imperative public importance" rule, once to settle the 1947 national coal strike and the other to declare unconstitutional President Truman's seizure of the steel mills during the Korean War. Even rarer were special terms of the court; there had been only four special terms in the court's history. If the court were to reject the request, and especially if it criticized the special prosecutor's action, "the psychological victory to the White House would be immeasurable." [47]

The White House in its brief opposing the expedited hearing, argued that "[a]ttempts in the past by the Court to make a hurried disposition of an important case arising in the dying days of a term have not been among the proudest chapters in the history of the Court." [48] The brief cited the Pentagon Papers case, in which Burger, Harlan, and Blackmun dissented, as "but the most recent example." The brief cited Burger's dissent in the case. The White House was "conspicuously wooing" the chief justice. [49] The White House was confident that its position would prevail. The court's calendar was full; the justices would have a ready excuse to sidestep the issue.

However, Leon Jaworski felt that if the prosecutors did not get a ruling quickly, the Watergate trial would be postponed repeatedly, with the government's case deteriorating and, perhaps, never going to trial at all. [50] Jaworski's gamble paid off; the Supreme Court granted his request and heard oral arguments on July 8.

3.3 White House Tapes Game
The Players and Their Strategies

When the justices went to conference on July 9, each of the eight who were to consider the case had basically two choices. They could either decide for or against the president. (Associate Justice Rehnquist apparently withdrew from the case because of his previous service at the Justice Department under John Mitchell, although he never publicly stated a reason for disqualifying himself.) It appears from the available record that six of the justices reached an early consensus against the president on all three of the major issues of whether or not the court had jurisdiction in the case since Jaworski was an employee of the executive branch, whether "executive privilege" was absolute, and whether or not Jaworski had demonstrated a sufficient need for the subpoenaed materials. [51]

Justices Burger and Blackmun, while concurring with the majority on limiting executive privilege, apparently believed that the special prosecutor lacked legal standing to sue the president.[52] For this reason, it appears, they voted originally against granting the case *certiorari*.[53]

Justices Burger and Blackmun are conceived of as one player. This is done because it is almost axiomatic that Blackmun voted with Burger. In the first five terms (1970 to 1974) that Burger and Blackmun served on the court, they agreed on 602 of the 721 cases they both heard (85.5 percent), which is the highest agreement level of any pair of justices who had served over these five terms.[54] They were referred to as the "Minnesota Twins" by the Supreme Court staff.

Justices Burger and Blackmun had a choice of two strategies:

1. Decide against the president on all major issues, joining the other six justices to create a unanimous decision.
2. Decide for the president on at least one major issue, forming a minority to create a 6–2 "weak" decision.

President Nixon's response to an adverse Supreme Court ruling was long a matter of doubt. On July 26, 1973, deputy White House press secretary Gerald Warren stated that president Nixon would abide by a "definitive decision of the highest court." Nixon endorsed the Warren formulation but neither he nor White House spokesmen would expand on the original statement. After the president had dismissed Cox and then agreed to submit the tapes that fall, the question of what "definitive" meant then became moot. The issue arose again on May 24, 1974 when Jaworski filed his appeal with the Supreme Court. The following day, presidential press secretary Ronald Zeigler was asked by reporters if the president still intended to obey a "definitive" Supreme Court ruling, Zeigler replied that he would not "speculate" on the president's actions and also declined to reaffirm the earlier statements by Warren and the president.[55]

Presidential spokesmen refused direct comment on the issue until July 9, when St. Clair made it clear that the president was at least keeping open the "option" of defying the court. The question of compliance, he stated, "has not yet been decided."[56]

Even in the oral arguments before the court on the previous day, St. Clair had strongly hinted at defiance. Justice Thurgood Marshall, in an exchange with St. Clair, had pressed the lawyer to admit that the issue of executive privilege was a legal question that was up to the Court to decide.

Marshall: And you are still leaving it up to this court to decide it?
St. Clair: Yes, in a sense.
Marshall: In what sense?
St. Clair: In the sense that this court has the obligation to determine the law. The President also has an obligation to carry out his constitutional duties.

            . . .

St. Clair: This is being submitted to this court for its guidance and judgment with respect to the law. The President, on the other hand, has his obligations under the Constitution.[57]

The implication of this exchange was that if the president did not agree with the "guidance" from the court, he might not obey its ruling. That is, the president would be looking for language in an opinion that would provide a rationale for defiance or, at most, severely limited compliance. St. Clair was saying that the court could decide the law but that the president would apply it. Philip Lacovara, who was arguing the case with Jaworski, noted Nixon's threat to defy the court. He concluded, ". . . we submit that this court should fully, explicitly and decisively . . . and *definitively* uphold Judge Sirica's opinion. . . ."[58] Thus, President Nixon had two strategies:

1. Comply with an adverse court ruling.
2. Defy an adverse court ruling.[59]

    Several factors help to explain President Nixon's refusal to make a definite commitment concerning his response to a court decision. If he stated that he would not comply, his statement might be used as a ground for impeachment. If he stated that he would comply, then the House Judiciary Committee might argue that the president would either have to comply with its subpoenas, too, or be impeached.[60]
    More importantly, though, the president's refusal to assure his compliance with an adverse decision was designed to

threaten the court and lead the justices to render either a favorable decision or, at worst, a closely divided adverse split decision which he could claim was insufficiently "definitive" for a matter of this magnitude. Woodward and Bernstein describe Nixon's reasoning as follows:

> A promise to comply would tempt the Court to rule against him Nixon had said. If the justices thought he was prepared to defy them, they might be less inclined to rule against him. Defiance would undermine the very basis of the Court's authority and create a constitutional crisis. And Nixon wanted to convey that threat.[61]

The threat backfired. According to Evans and Novak, "The refusal of St. Clair to say Nixon would obey an adverse decision has disturbed the judicial branch from the high court down."[62] The threat of defiance put severe pressure on the justices to hand down a unanimous opinion in an effort to muster all the court's prestige for a possible confrontation with the president. Historically, the Supreme Court has tended to produce strong or unanimous decisions in major constitutional cases even when opinion within the court is really divided. For example, in the 1954 *Brown* school desegregation decision, the court split 6–3 in its deliberations only to present a unanimous ruling to the nation.[63]

The Outcomes and Their Rankings by the Players
The possible outcomes of the four possible strategy choices of the two players are presented in Figure 3.1.

If the president defied the court, his defiance would represent a direct assault on the Supreme Court's constitutional place as the principal source and final authority of constitutional interpretation and thereby threaten the very structure of the American political system. In fact, not only the confrontation over the tapes, but also all that has come to be included under the rubric "Watergate," is seen by some as a product of Nixon's drive toward an "imperial presidency." In so characterizing Nixon's presidency, Arthur Schlesinger, Jr. argues that Nixon was "heading toward a new balance of constitutional powers, an audacious and imaginative reconstruction of the American constitution."[64]

FIGURE 3.1
OUTCOME MATRIX OF THE WHITE HOUSE TAPES GAME

NIXON

	COMPLY WITH COURT	DEFY COURT
BURGER and BLACKMUN — Decide for president; create a "weak" 6-2 decision	A. Constitutional crisis averted; Nixon not impeached for non-compliance; majority-rule principle preserved.	B. Constitutional crisis; Nixon impeached but conviction uncertain.
Decide against president; create a unanimous 8-0 decision.	C. Constitutional crisis averted; Nixon not impeached for non-compliance; majority rule possibly weakened.	D. Constitutional crisis; Nixon impeached and conviction certain.

NOTE: The only impeachment charge being considered here is noncompliance with the Supreme Court decision on the tapes, not any of the other charges voted by the House Judiciary Committee in July 1974.

If Nixon had attempted to redefine (usurp) the Supreme Court's prerogatives through outright defiance, it seems highly probable that he would have plunged the country into its deepest constitutional crisis since the Civil War. No previous president had ever explicitly defied an order of the Supreme Court, though such action had apparently been contemplated.[65] Franklin Roosevelt, for one, reportedly was prepared to defy the court in order "to protect that economic and political security of this nation" in the 1935 "Gold" case when the court was expected to rule that the government was required to redeem bonds in gold.[66] According to Arthur Schlesinger, Jr., Roosevelt had prepared "a dissent of his own in the shape of a set of proclamations and orders nullifying an adverse Supreme Court decision."[67] A surprise 5-4 verdict in favor of the president's position made Roosevelt's contemplated actions unnecessary.

More than a century earlier, in 1832, Andrew Jackson had sharply objected to a ruling that federal authorities, rather than the state of Georgia, should assume jurisdiction over the case of a missionary to the Cherokee Indians who was imprisoned by the state. Jackson reputedly remarked after the court decided against him, "Well, John Marshall has made his decision; now let him enforce it." That ruling, however, did not specifically require Jackson to take any action.[68] Jackson's comment pinpoints the crux of all confrontations between the president and the Supreme Court. The court has no physical means to execute its decisions. Its power resides in the near-universal acceptance of the doctrine of "judicial supremacy". According to former Associate Justice Robert Jackson,

> The people have seemed to feel that the Supreme Court, whatever its defects, is still the more detached, dispassionate, and trustworthy custodian that our system affords for the translation of abstract ideas into concrete constitutional commands.[69]

Thus, while the president could ignore the Supreme Court,

> . . . he would rationally do so only if he had substantial Congressional support for such an action. Equally important for a President would be the distinction between public and Congressional disapproval of a particular judicial decision, on the one hand, and public and Congressional approval of Presidential defiance of the Court, on the other.[70]

President Nixon lacked such substantial support in his challenge to the court. At the time of the decision in *United States* v. *Nixon*, it appeared that the result of presidential defiance would be impeachment by the House of Representatives. Representative Lawrence Hogan, a Maryland Republican and member of the House Judiciary Committee, framed the result of defiance in its extreme form: "We could almost impeach him by unanimous consent in the House. . . . He would be impeached in the committee 38 to 0."[71] Even Vice President Ford, who had been travelling around the country on the president's behalf and contending that the prospect of impeachment was diminishing, conceded that defiance of the court would create "a whole new ball game."[72]

The outcome in the Senate was less certain than in the House. Although the Constitution requires only a simple majority in the House to impeach it requires a two-thirds majority in the Senate to convict and remove a president from office. This meant that any 34 Senators could keep the president in office. To attain the necessary 34 votes, the White House adopted a technique that came to be known as "impeachment politics," which involved "a tailoring, of the Nixon Administration's foreign and domestic policy so as to appeal to that combination of southern Democrats and conservative Republicans who made up . . . a hard 34 votes in the Senate."[73] In part, this technique hinged on the support of the more conservative Senators against what the White House had long argued was a partisan purge by the president's liberal "enemies."[74]

Herein lies the differential impact of a unanimous versus a "weak" decision. A weak decision from which at least some of the justices dissented would allow the president to continue his "one-third plus one" strategy in the Senate. (More immediately, a weak decision might lead the president to defy the court. Leon Jaworski believed that if the decision went against the president by a close vote, he "would go on television and tell the people that the presidency should not be impaired by a divided court."[75]) A unanimous adverse ruling that included three conservative Nixon appointees would preempt charges that the president was the victim of what presidential counsellor Dean Burch called a "partisan lynch mob."[76] The final minority report of the ten Republican "stalwarts" on the House Judiciary

Committee who had voted against impeachment indicates the effect of a unanimous decision:

> We know it has been said, and perhaps some will continue to say, that Richard Nixon was "hounded from office" by his political opponents and media critics. We feel constrained to point out, however, that it was Richard Nixon, who impeded the FBI's investigation of the Watergate affair by wrongfully attempting to implicate the Central Intelligence Agency; it was Richard Nixon who created and preserved evidence of that transgression and who, *knowing that it had been subpoenaed by this committee and the Special Prosecutor*, concealed its terrible import, even from his own counsel, until he could do so no longer. And it was a unanimous Supreme Court of the United States which, in an opinion authored by the Chief Justice whom he appointed, ordered Richard Nixon to surrender that evidence to further the ends of justice.[77]

Defying a unanimous decision would, in all probability, ignite a "firestorm" of protest that would dwarf the one following the firing of Archibald Cox as special prosecutor and inexorably lead to the president's impeachment, conviction, and removal from office. (This feeling was apparently shared by James St. Clair who, on the morning of the decision, warned the president that he would be surely impeached and swiftly convicted if he were to defy the unanimous ruling of the court.)[78]

Compliance with any adverse Supreme Court decision would avert a constitutional crisis, and President Nixon would avoid immediate impeachment in the House on the ground of withholding evidence from the special prosecutor and/or violation of the separation-of-powers principle. However, compliance posed problems for the president; the subpoenaed materials, if released, could prove fatal to his impeachment defense in Congress. Indeed, upon learning of the court's decision, Nixon, who was at San Clemente, telephoned White House special counsel Fred Buzhardt in Washington: "There may be some problems with the June 23 tape," Nixon said.[79]

Although the revelation of this tape ultimately forced his resignation, President Nixon apparently did not fully realize at the time the incriminating nature of the recorded conversations. Woodward and Bernstein report that Buzhardt felt that the tape was "devastating"; Nixon, in contrast, felt that Buzhardt was "overreacting," that it was "not that bad."[80] Even as late as August 5, in his statement accompanying the public release of the tape transcripts, Nixon reflected his mixed evaluation of the tape's impact, that "this additional material I am now furnishing may further damage my case. . . . I am firmly convinced that the record, in its entirety, does not justify the extreme step of impeachment and removal from office."[81]

Compliance, or more accurately, the announcement of compliance, would allow the president to fall back on his long-used strategy of delay. In the statement announcing the president's compliance, St. Clair concluded: ". . . the time-consuming process of reviewing the tapes . . . and the preparation of the index and analysis required by Judge Sirica's order will begin forthwith."[82] St. Clair had previously indicated that it might take as long as a month to prepare the tapes.[83]

Thus, compliance would buy time for the president, though it would not necessarily remove the threat of impeachment and ultimate conviction, expecially if the court were unanimous in its judgment. For Justices Burger and Blackmun, to support the majority (apparently against their convictions) to counter a presumed threat might possibly weaken the majority-rule principle that *any* majority is sufficient for a ("definitive") decision.[84] But voting their (presumed) convictions would be hazardous should the president use a divided decision as an excuse to defy the court.

These conflicting considerations are now combined into a rank ordering of the four outcomes by the two players.

Clearly, President Nixon preferred the *risk* of conviction and removal to its virtual certainty. Thus, the president would prefer to defy a weak decision (outcome B in Figure 3.1) than to defy a unanimous decision (D); hence (B,D). For the same reason, he would prefer to comply with any adverse decision (A or C) than to defy a unanimous decision (D), his worst outcome; hence (A-C,D).

Defying a weak decision (B) is considered preferable to complying with any adverse decision (A or C), for such defiance would preclude the release of potentially devastating evidence and at the same time present Nixon with the possibility of avoiding conviction and removal for noncompliance; hence (B,A-C). Between the two compliance outcomes (A and B), it is assumed that the president "preferred" to comply with a weak decision (A) than with a unanimous decision (C); hence (A,C). A weak decision with some justices dissenting would leave the issue confused and subject to interpretation; a weak decision would leave room to maneuver for partial compliance.[85]

Putting the partial preference scales together, the president's presumed ranking of the four outcomes (from best to worst), defined by the two strategies of each player (where subscript, N, represents Nixon and subscript, BB, represent Burger and Blackmun), is:

B. Defy_N/Decide for_{BB};

A. Comply_N/Decide for_{BB};

C. Comply_N/Decide against_{BB};

D. Defy_N/Decide against_{BB}.

Given these rankings by the president, what are the corresponding rankings of Justices Burger and Blackmun?

Although it was previously suggested that Burger and Blackmun would have preferred to decide for the president on at least one of the strictly legal questions (standing to sue by the special prosecutor), there is no doubt that the justices believed that compliance by the president with any adverse court ruling (A or C) would be preferable to defiance (B or D); hence (A-C,B-D). Indeed, in the court's opinion, which Burger drafted, the chief justice quoted Chief Justice John Marshall in *Marbury* v. *Madison* (1803): "It is emphatically the province and duty of the Judicial department to say what the law is."

It also seems reasonable to assume that if the president complies (A or C), the justices would prefer to decide for him (A) rather than against him (C); hence (A,C). After all, the notion that the court must be unanimous or close to it to make a decision credible, and thereby induce compliance, is an undesirable restriction on the court's authority. A unanimous decision, if perceived to be the result of presidential intimidation, might establish an unhealthy precedent, for

. . . when the Court's decisions even appear to have been influenced by Congress or the President, the constitutional separation of powers doctrine is violated, the independence of the Court is compromised and the integrity of the court is damaged.[86]

Finally, we assume that the justices "preferred" the president to defy a unanimous decision (D) to his defying a weak decision (B), hence (D,B). That is, should the president defy the court or say that he would, the justices would prefer to confront him with a unanimous decision rather than provide him with a pretext upon which to defy the court and thereby precipitate a constitutional crisis.

Combining the partial preference scales, the justices' presumed ranking of the four outcomes (from best to worst) is:

A. Decide for$_{BB}$/Comply$_N$;

C. Decide against$_{BB}$/Comply$_N$;

D. Decide against$_{BB}$/Comply$_N$;

B. Decide for$_{BB}$/Defy$_N$.

If we represent the best outcome for each player by "4," the next-best by "3," and so on, the rankings of the four outcomes in the Figure 3.1 outcome matrix are shown in the Figure 3.2 payoff matrix.

The Game Tree and its Normal-Form Representation

Because the players in the White House tapes game did not make simultaneous choices in ignorance of each other, the payoff matrix in Figure 3.2 does not provide a complete representation of this game. Justices Burger and Blackmun—and the court—acted first, and only then did President Nixon have to make a strategy choice, as depicted in the *game tree* in Figure 3.3. (read from top to bottom).

The game tree shows that Burger and Blackmun had two choices open to them, and, depending on how the court ruled, there were four possible choices open to Nixon. That is, before the court rendered its verdict, any of the four outcomes could occur.

The payoffs associated with these outcomes are shown as the endpoints of the four lower branches of the game tree in Figure 3.3.

Figure 3.4 presents the *normal-form*, or matrix, representation of this game, wherein Burger and Blackmun have two

FIGURE 3.2
PAYOFF MATRIX OF WHITE HOUSE TAPES GAME

NIXON

		COMPLY WITH COURT	DEFY COURT
BURGER and	Decide for president	A. 4,3	B. 1,4
BLACKMUN	Decide against president	C. 3,2	D. 2,1

NOTE: 1. x, y = Burger and Blackmun, Nixon.
2. Neither Burger and Blackmun nor Nixon have a dominant strategy; none of the outcomes is in equilibrium. There is no rational outcome.

strategies, but Nixon now has four strategies. This is so because each of Nixon's two original strategies, "comply" and "defy," are contingent on what Burger and Blackmun decide ("Decide for president," "Decide against president"), which yields 2 × 2 = 4 strategies for the president.

FIGURE 3.3
GAME TREE OF WHITE HOUSE TAPES GAME

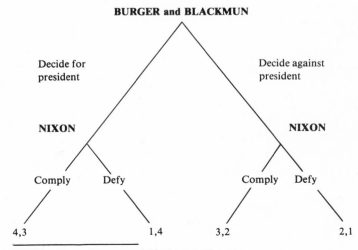

NOTE: x, y = Burger and Blackmun, Nixon.

The payoffs in Figure 3.4 can be derived from the payoffs given in either Figure 3.2 or Figure 3.3. For example, assume Burger and Blackmun choose "decide against the president," and Nixon chooses "comply if Burger and Blackmun decide against, defy if Burger and Blackmun decide for." Since Burger and Blackmun choose to "decide against the president," this choice implies that Nixon's choice will be to "comply" which yields the payoff (3,2) associated with "Decide against president/Comply" outcome in both the payoff matrix of Figure 3.2 and the game tree of Figure 3.3.

Now let us turn to the analysis of the White House tapes game shown in Figure 3.4. It is easy to show that "defy if decide for, comply if decide against" is a *dominant strategy* for Nixon: It yields payoffs as good as, and in at least one case better than, the payoffs yielded by any of his other three strategies, whatever the strategy choice of Burger and Blackmun.

Given this unconditionally best strategy choice on the part of Nixon, it is reasonable to assume that Burger and Blackmun will anticipate its choice, assuming they (as well as Nixon) have complete information about the Figure 3.4 payoff matrix. To maximize their payoff, Burger and Blackmun will choose the strategy which yields for them the highest payoff in that column associated with Nixon's dominant strategy (the fourth column in Figure 3.4). Since "3" is better than "1" for Burger and Blackmun in this column, we would therefore expect that they would choose to "decide against the president."

In fact, as we already know, the Supreme Court did decide unanimously against President Nixon. The eight justices, because of necessity to write a "definitive" opinion and support it unanimously came down on Jaworski's side of every issue—jurisdiction, executive privilege, separation of powers, and confidentiality. Nixon was reportedly shocked by the court's ruling, feeling himself "sold out" by his three appointees, Chief Justice Burger and Associate Justices Blackmun and Powell.[87] Charles Colson claims that the president counted on all three justices. Others say he was certain of only Burger and Blackmun. When he learned of the decision, Nixon used expletive-deleted language to describe Burger. The president could not believe that the court's ruling had been unanimous. "Significantly, the pres-

FIGURE 3.4
NORMAL-FORM OF WHITE HOUSE TAPES GAME

NIXON

BURGER and BLACKMUN	COMPLY (C) REGARDLESS	DEFY (D) REGARDLESS	C if F, D if A	D if F, C if A
Decide for president (F)	4,3	1,4	4,3	1,4
Decide against president (A)	3,2	2,1	2,1	(3,2)

Nixon has dominant strategy.

Burger and Blackmun anticipating Nixon's dominant strategy, decide against the president.

NOTE: 1. x, y = Burger and Blackmun, Nixon.

2. The circled outcome 3,2 is in equilibrium; Nixon's "D if F, C if A" ("Defy if decide for, comply if decide against") strategy is dominant.

ident's greatest fury seems to have been directed not at the decision itself but at the three justices who 'deserted' him."[88]

In any event, the decision was unanimous with no dissenting or concurring opinions. "It was the Court's seamless unity which made defiance so difficult."[89] Nixon has revealed in his memoirs that he hoped and felt that the Supreme Court would not rule against him, but he had been prepared to defy any adverse Supreme Court decision that had any "air" in it. If he were to "abide" by an adverse decision, this would consist of "releasing tapes in excerpted form."[90]

Eight hours after the decision was handed down, the president, through St. Clair, announced his compliance with the decision "in all respects." The justices, contrary to H. R. Haldeman's view that they had "unknowingly" averted a "supremely critical confrontation" between the president and the court, acted quite calculatingly and rationally to maintain the integrity of the court.[91]

In summary, the game-theoretic analysis seems to retrodict well, in terms of the reconstruction of the players' strategies and preferences for outcomes, why the players acted as they did.

3.4 A Paradox of Rational Choice[92]

It is worth noting that the payoff (3,2) associated with the strategies "decide against the president" and "defy if decide for, comply if decide against" is not only the outcome one would expect on the basis of the reasoning presented earlier but also it is the only outcome in Figure 3.4 that is *in equilibrium*: Once chosen by both players, neither player has an incentive to depart unilaterally from it because he will do no better, and perhaps worse, if he does. Yet, paradoxically, *both* players could have been better off if they had chosen strategies associated with either of the two (4,3) payoffs in the Figure 3.4 matrix. The outcomes that yield these payoffs both involve the choice by Burger and Blackmun of deciding for the president, and the choice by Nixon of compliance. The president can "arrive at" this choice either by selecting "comply regardless' or "comply if decide for, defy if decide against" in the Figure 3.4 matrix.

Unfortunately for the players, however, neither of the outcomes that yield (4,3) as a payoff is in equilibrium: Nixon in each case has an incentive to depart unilaterally from the strategies associated with (4,3) to try to bring about his best outcome, (1,4). Not only are the (4,3) outcomes not in equilibrium, but Nixon's two strategies associated with these outcomes are dominated by his (dominant) strategy, "defy if decide for, comply if decide against."[93]

For reasons just given, therefore, it is hard to see how both players could have done better, even though the opportunity existed. This situation is reminiscent of the classic 2 × 2 Prisoner's Dilemma game in which the single equilibrium outcome is nonPareto-optimal but, nonetheless, the product of dominant strategy choices by both players (not just one, as in the White House tapes game).[94]

Like the Prisoner's Dilemma, however, it is conceivable that if the players had been willing to trust each other a bit more, they could have avoided "locking into" the noncooperative outcome (3,2). Specifically, if Burger and Blackmun had believed that had they dissented Nixon would not defy the court, they could have voted their (presumed) convictions with greater equanimity.

This logic is theoretically supported by metagame theory.[95] The metagame expansion of Burger and Blackmun's two strategies to 16 metastrategies, contingent on Nixon's four strategies in Figure 3.4, reveals them to have a dominant metastrategy that includes (4,3) as an equilibrium outcome.[96] Its normative interpretation is that Burger and Blackmun should decide for the president if and only if they believe he will choose "comply regardless" or "comply if decide for, defy if decide against." This conditional response on the part of the two justices implies a tit-for-tat kind of thinking: "We will support you if we are assured that you will comply with the Court, even if the decision is not unanimous; otherwise, we won't."

The public record indicates that neither Burger, Blackman, nor any other justice ever received such assurance from the president. Quite the contrary; Nixon and his spokesmen, as we indicated earlier, continually held out the possibility of defying a Supreme Court decision that was not "definitive." Thus, even at a metagame-theoretic level, Burger and Blackmun had no choice—despite their disagreement with some arguments of the special prosecutor—but to decide against the president. Thereby the Supreme Court decision was rendered unanimous and both players in the White House tapes game lost out, in a sense, on greater payoffs that—at least in principle—were attainable.

If we include nonplayers as interested parties, however, they may of course benefit from a "noncooperative" solution. For example, it seems likely that the special prosecutor in the White House tapes case would rank the outcome that actually occurred as the best of the four possible outcomes. This is certainly a reasonable inference from Jaworski's remarks immediately after the court decision "I feel right good over what happened. . . . I'm especially pleased it was a unanimous decision. It doesn't leave a doubt in anyone's mind."[97]

3.5 Impact of the Supreme Court Decision

The Supreme Court ruling was devastating to the president's position in Congress. By mid-July, the White House had succeeded in slowing the pro-impeachment momentum of the House Judiciary Committee.[98] Until the decision, the White House and its supporters had denounced the Judiciary Committee as a prejudiced, political jury. Political pressures were being brought to bear to be "loyal" to the president and the Republican party. Impeachment would be converted into a partisan contest by polarizing first the House Judiciary Committee, then the House, and ultimately, if necessary, the Senate.[99]

The court changed the nature of the issue. It made opposition to the president not only legal but respectable as well. After the decision, some of the House members considered as "undecideds" spoke openly of possibly casting their votes for impeachment.[100]

On the day after the decision, James Reston analyzed the effect of the court's decision:

> The Supreme Court has changed the atmosphere, and maybe even the balance of power, in the impeachment debate in the Congress. . . . For the last few difficult weeks, the swing votes

in the House and Senate, the worriers and doubters, have not known what to do, but the Supreme Court without even mentioning 'impeachment' has given them a lead. By a unanimous decision, it has said, just when the whole debate was going on television, follow the evidence, turn over the tapes, let's get the facts.[101]

3.6 Epilogue

This chapter was originally written, and parts of it published, before Bob Woodward and Scott Armstrong's *The Brethren*—the most extensive inside view of the Supreme Court ever written—appeared.[102] This book deals extensively with the White House tapes case, providing material germane to the preceding analysis. Woodward and Armstrong have been seriously criticized for their exclusive reliance on anonymous sources, the use of third-hand hearsay, and their inaccuracies regarding the court's procedure and historical fact.[103] Nonetheless, given its best-seller status and its use in academia, *The Brethren* represents the "conventional wisdom" on the court in the White House tapes case and, therefore, should be noted. Thus, the original chapter was not rewritten (and this section added) for two reasons: first, questions of accuracy and, second, to "test" the analysis made above.

If it is assumed that *The Brethren* is *totally* accurate, it seems that some of the assumptions made above, based on the then-available evidence, were incorrect, but that the major thrust of the analysis holds up quite well.

Woodward and Armstrong report that the vote on granting Jaworski's certiorari request was 6–2, with Blackmun and White in opposition. The two justices believed, as the White House had argued, that there was a danger in a Supreme Court "rush to judgment," of a "hasty ill-conceived decision" like that in the Pentagon Papers case.[104] White in particular believed that the justices should "let the case mature and come to the court naturally."[105] Blackmun wanted to ensure that the court did not act "recklessly" by expediting the coverup trial when there was not "sufficient cause to depart from normal practice."[106]

According to Woodward and Armstrong, Burger at first

stated that he "had problems expediting the case. . . . All that was at stake was a possible delay in the cover-up trial . . . hardly a matter of national emergency."[107] Only after the issue was decided, with five justices voting to take the case immediately, did Burger side with the majority.

After hearing oral arguments, Woodward and Armstrong report that the court appeared to be close to unanimity on the broad outlines of the opinion. (It does not appear that either Burger or Blackmun doubted the special prosecutor's standing to sue.) Unanimity, without dissents or concurring opinions, was felt by all to be absolutely essential. According to Woodward and Armstrong, Justice Brennan believed that a unanimous opinion would be "the greatest deterrent to a defiant President. . . . The Court could erupt into a confusing mixture of opinions, concurrences and dissents. Without reconciliation, Richard Nixon might find a loophole."[108]

The justices, as was assumed, were concerned with preserving the institutional prerogatives of the court. "Conversation at conference normally focused on a case in light of the Constitution. The conference discussion had centered more on the Court's role and power than on the case."[109] Justice Stewart is said to have believed the following:

> The Court's authority was now the issue. The president had made it one. This business about obeying only a 'definitive' opinion was a challenge. Court rulings had to be obeyed, definitive or not. Compliance was not a matter for a President to decide.[110]

Despite the general agreement, significant differences separated the justices on the form and content of the opinion, particularly Burger and the other seven. However, Burger declared that the tapes case, like *Brown*, "needed" the chief justice—and claimed it as his own.[111]

Burger had often shown himself to be motivated by what the other justices felt were crass, overt political considerations. Burger was viewed by his colleagues as an unabashed Nixon loyalist who ruled against administration policy only when it was necessary to save face. Some of Burger's opinions read like Nixon administration press releases to his colleagues.[112]

Burger shared Nixon's view that Watergate was simply

a partisan vendetta to reverse the 1972 electoral mandate. He saw the news media as involved in a "witch hunt"; the newspapers were "character assassins" employing innuendo, distortion and hearsay.[113] Burger was blind to the seriousness of Watergate. "Apart from the morality I don't see what they [Nixon, his aides and associates] did wrong."[114]

When Burger's draft opinion was circulated, the other justices found it appalling. Several threatened to dissent. Three justices—Brennan, White and Stewart—seemed to agree that "the Chief wanted to scuttle the opinion."[115] To Justice Stewart, "Nixon was desperate. Surely he would look for any ambiguity or favorable point on which to base a last ditch defense."[116] Burger's draft would have provided such a defense; it "invited anarchy."[117]

The other justices then embarked on a "coup" in which each proposed alternative drafts to various sections of Burger's opinions. In the end, bowing to the other justices, Burger wrote a new draft opinion that borrowed from Blackmun on the facts, Stewart on the authority of the judiciary, White on the reach of the subpoena power, Powell on presidential confidentiality, Brennan on the special prosecutor's standing to sue for the tapes, William O. Douglas on whether such a suit could be appealed to the Supreme Court, and some footnote changes by Thurgood Marshall. But one problem that remained related to the section dealing with Nixon's claim that the tapes were guarded from disclosure by executive privilege. Burger argued that the privilege did have constitutional validity. But, creating a new bit of constitutional law, he wrote that the privilege had to give way in this case because the "core functions" of the judiciary were involved (that is, the courts needed the tapes as evidence) whereas, those of the executive branch were not.[118]

Several of the justices saw the "core functions" approach as unsound and extremely dangerous and rewrote the section. By the afternoon of July 22, the other seven justices reached agreement on a rewrite of the disputed section made by Stewart and sent it to Burger with an ultimatum: include it in the opinion or they would withhold their votes. The chief justice was the only holdout to his own opinion.[119] Burger felt "sandbagged" by the other justices but "he wanted [the decision] to be unanimous".[120]

The next morning the chief justice circulated a revised draft of the most controversial section, dropping the most threatening points and incorporating the substance of the Stewart proposal. After some doubts by Powell and Douglas were proposed and quickly withdrawn, the draft was accepted by the eight justices. The opinion would be unanimous, with no "air" for Nixon to exploit.

Thus, the original chapter incorrectly included Burger as a dissenter in granting certiorari (although his concurrence is suspect) and mistook Blackmun's reasons for his dissent. Also, neither Burger nor Blackmun in the period after oral arguments appear to have questioned Jaworski's "standing." However, Woodward and Armstrong confirm the justices' intense concern with unanimity as a means to preserve the court's integrity in the face of the president's threat of noncompliance. Also, Burger did represent the president's best hope for an opinion that would provide him the necessary "loopholes" upon which to base his defiance or minimal compliance.

Essentially, then, if the original chapter were rewritten, a "weak" decision would be defined as a 7–1 decision, with Burger filing a dissent or a concurrence or a decision that, although unanimous, would provide the president a rationale for defiance. Indeed, Burger's draft opinion would have provided Nixon ample room to maneuver.

To get an image of the game, each [the player and the observer] has to resort to guesswork, hypothesis and inference as well as observation. The only test of the validity of the image is its plausibility.

John McDonald, *The Game of Business*

In the analysis of any historical phenomenon there will always be debate about how much to attribute to the influence of individuals and how much to attribute to general forces of a material or ideal nature. Watergate is no different.

Paul Halpern, *Why Watergate?*

Conclusion

In this chapter, I shall evaluate the application of game theory to Watergate, emphasizing the advantages of the use of a rigorous theoretical framework in the analysis of complex historical events. I shall also assess Richard Nixon's decision-making in Watergate, discussing the salient factors that affected the quality of his choices.

An Evaluation of the Theory[1]

To me, the preceding analysis demonstrates that the positing of Watergate figures as players in games is natural, providing both "plausible" images of the events examined and sound interpretations of them. This is clearly confirmed, I believe, by the ability of the theory to structure incomplete or contradictory information such as in the White House tapes game and to reach conclusions that hold up quite well when significant new evidence becomes available.

Certainly what is "natural" or "plausible" can be disputed; some may consider aspects of the analysis incomplete and, in some cases, strained. However, it must be remembered that I do not claim to capture every nuance of character motivation nor have I tried to enumerate all possible choices available to Watergate players in a payoff matrix or a game tree. It was not my intention to present an exhaustive disquisition on Watergate or even a complete examination of the three "games" chosen. Rather, I attempted to delineate the most important strategic elements of these historically crucial situations and employed game theory as a tool to analyze and explain them.

Game theory's focus on strategic choice enables the investigator to pull together observations and interpretations into a set of coherent patterns rather than to settle for a series of unrelated and discursive statements. It avoids the "levels of analysis" problem alluded to by Halpern in the epigram quote. The notion of strategy forces a consideration and integration of the psychological, institutional, societal, and systemic factors that influence a player's choice.

The focus on strategy necessarily depends on my interpretation of character motivations. Although game theory is not a "theory of value"—it does not directly speak to the formulation of goals–it does provide a rigorous framework for relating and interpreting actions by its use of such concepts as "rationality," "strategy," "outcome," and "payoff." Without these conceptual tools, it would be far more difficult to ascertain the "true" motivations of Watergate players. The raw public record is too disputatious, providing no criteria for choice among competing interpretations.

Although few, if any, of the Watergate players knew game theory (except, perhaps, Elliot Richardson), I would argue that their conduct was game-theoretic.[2] That is, the theory offers an understanding of what they were doing when they did it.

The formulation of strategies, and their elucidation by the analyst, is obviously difficult and of critical importance. While the preferences of Watergate figures are often clear, the strategies they chose to implement them are often inchoate. This difficulty in determining the strategic content of the decisions and actions of Watergate participants results from the "submerged"[3] nature of the play of the games; much of all the games is "played in the head." Where the documenting record is nonexistent, unclear, or contradictory, I attempted to present alternative interpretations of character motivation and of available choices and assess their consequences.

The power of game theory in the Watergate analysis lies not only in the fact that we can use it to provide a point of view, and to organize information around it, but also to discriminate among various motivational assumptions that work and do not work to explain the events that occurred. For example, an examination of Elliot Richardson's choice of strategies, and his efforts to structure the events that led to the Saturday Night Massacre, led me to draw certain inferences as to his motives.

Specifically, an examination of his interaction with Cox and the game he played with the White House suggested his reputation as an exemplar of the "public man of conscience" to be exaggerated.

It may be objected that game theory may "work" well for some Watergate situations but not for others and, in particular, that the situations I chose were atypical or selected because they somehow "fit" the theory. Obviously, selective criteria were used to determine the specific form of the reconstructions of the situations I analyzed (that is, who were the important players, that were their available strategies, what were the possible outcomes, how the outcomes were ranked). But, I would argue, the games analyzed in the previous chapters are not only historically crucial but also that my reconstruction faithfully captures the historical strategic elements. This is not to say that other games could not have been chosen using the "historically crucial" criterion. For example, an "Ervin Committee" or an "Impeachment" game are possibilities. Nor is it to say that other analysts using more advanced game theory than the equilibrium and dominant strategy approach employed here could not significantly refine and expand our understanding of Watergate.

Even if it is granted that the scope and organizing power of game theory is broad and its application to Watergate natural and plausible, the question remains, "Does it provide insights difficult to perceive without the clarification of the theory?" It does in two ways. First, as we have seen, it discriminates between motivational assumptions that work. Second, it provides a vocabulary and a calculus that illuminate common themes in different decision-making situations. For example, the game between Nixon and the Supreme Court (Figure 3.4) elucidates the dilemmas that confront rational players in real-life games. In this game, the rational outcome was inferior to one of the possible outcomes for both players but that this mutually better outcome was not stable.

The theory also highlights other paradoxes of rational behavior. For example, in the "Silbert Ploy" it was demonstrated that a player is sometimes better off being ignorant and deceived. Additionally, the theory clearly explicated the necessary and sufficient conditions under which deception can be accomplished.

The presentation of games in interrelated sequences, where the outcome of one game significantly alters both subsequent and concurrent games, demonstrates the dynamic potentialities of the theory. It was shown that the outcomes of prior games directly changed the strategy choices available to the players and the value the players imputed to the outcomes in subsequent games. An example of this dependence is the impact of the McCord defection game and the "Silbert Ploy" game on the Dean-Magruder game. The outcomes of the former games are the central elements of the latter game. Although each game remains a static snapshot, several snapshots shown in sequence create a movie.

Game-theoretic analysis can have a prescriptive dimension. For example, such analysis may help policy makers avoid dilemmas of the kind illustrated by the White House tapes and Dean-Magruder games that work to the disadvantage of all players. Such problematic games seem pervasive in the real world, and understanding the dilemmas they give rise to—and how they may be avoided—is a first step in carrying out useful policy analyses.

Game theory's focus on alternative strategies and alternative outcomes allows the analyst to demonstrate rigorously what outcomes might have resulted if different strategies were chosen by the players. That is, the theory is "retroactively prescriptive," meaning it can demonstrate what choices should have been chosen by players to achieve their goals. For example, in the Saturday Night Massacre game, it was shown that if the president had not included a prohibition on access in the basic "Stennis compromise," it would have been much more difficult, if not impossible, for Cox to induce Richardson to desert the president. Also, in the White House tapes game, if the president had not threatened defiance of a "nondefinitive" decision, the justices might not have felt the compulsion to produce the "airtight" decision they did. Indeed, if the decision had instead been "weak," as we have seen, the president might have been provided with grounds for outright defiance or severely circumscribed compliance.

Game theory can elucidate the norms of behavior of players in a way not possible by other means. For example, observers of the Supreme Court have suggested that "threats" to the court induce unanimous or lopsided majorities. However, as the authors of the best analysis of this proposition, Spaeth and Rodhe, admit, it seems impossible "to derive an objective indicator of threat situations."[4] The White House tapes game demonstrated how the norm of unanimity can be derived as a consequence of rational choices by the justices in a particular case.

Finally, a word on rationality. In each game, it has been initially assumed that the players were rational. The players' rational strategies as suggested by game theory, and the outcomes associated with these choices, were then compared to the choices actually made. Thereby, the correspondence of the game-theoretic model and the events that occurred historically could be ascertained. The correspondence in the games analyzed was high, suggesting that the major Watergate participants' behavior was purposeful, at least with respect to preferences it is plausible to assume they held. There was nothing bizarre or psychotic about the behavior of Watergate characters, who did their best, under the circumstances, to extricate themselves from a bad situation that became intractable. The Watergate players as seen here are quite ordinary people calculating, as best they could, how to minimize the "damage". These people were *not* irrational; their actions *did* seem to them, on the basis of careful and prolonged consideration, to be the best means to avert disaster.

Thus, I believe that the analysis demonstrates that game theory provides a valuable framework within which significant complex historical situations can be explained—in the rigorous sense of the word—in a way not possible by other approaches.

An Assessment of Richard Nixon

The Richard Nixon portrayed in the previous chapters is a man who acted rationally in response to events and to actions by other Watergate players. Nonetheless, he fell. Why? Simply, Richard Nixon was playing a game with severe constraints on his decision-making. These constraints included the nature of his goals, his personality and style, his own previous decisions, environmental constraints such as restrictions on information and communication, the rules of the judicial "game," and "chance."

Personality, Goals, and Strategy

Personality and character structure goals; goals, in turn, structure the form rationality takes, or strategy. To evaluate the "quality" of Richard Nixon's decision-making it is necessary to understand, at least in broad outline, relationships among these factors.[5]

I do not intend to review exhaustively the psychological literature on Richard Nixon but rather present that which appears to be most salient to an explanation of his Watergate behavior.[6] According to James David Barber, Nixon had an "active-negative" character. The overriding aim of the active-negative president is to "get and keep power"[7] In psychological terms, Barber sees Nixon substituting technique for value.[8] His focus is on procedure—on the *how* rather than the *what*. Richard Nixon's goals were not defined by political principles, ethics, or morality but by what could be termed "Lombardi's Law," "Winning isn't everything; it's the only thing." To Nixon what is needed is not principled goals but the "will to win."[9]

The overriding focus on "power" and "winning" are elements of what has been termed a "hyperstrategic" mentality.[10] As we have seen, rationality and strategy are concerned with procedure and process. They enable you to go from where you are to where you want to go; they allow you to maximize the achievement of your goals. Strategic theories are emphatically not "theories of value." The proper employment of strategy helps decision-makers attain concrete objectives that are defined by other values.

However, there is the danger that the process *becomes* the goal. That is, "success" is defined not as maximizing intrinsic values but as augmenting means. Hence, power for the sake of power, success for the sake of success, and winning for the sake of winning become the goals. Instrumental objectives such as electroral performance, image construction, and high poll ratings, for example, become paramount.[11] Perversely, goals become defined by exclusively strategic considerations rather than the reverse.

Nixon appears to have had a hyperstrategic mentality in the Watergate affair. His focus was on process. According to Barber, Nixon does not act from a defined political or philosophical position to deal with issues. Rather, he attains office and, lacking external goals, waits for his political role to present a problem to him.[12]

Nixon viewed the world as people by ruthless enemies out to destroy him. To him, the political world is zero-sum. What you win, you win from someone and what you lose, you lose to someone. In this world opponents become enemies against whom any means, legal or illegal, become justified, indeed, necessary. Since opponents are perceived to be thinking the same way, the behavioral rule becomes "do unto others before they do unto you." Politics is war as Nixon constantly reminded his associates.[13] In this context, those who planned and executed the Watergate break-in acted rationally given their paramount goal of winning.

For Nixon, immediate tactical achievements replaced larger values and, often, long-range expediency. Thus, Nixon could act rationally, "win" in the short run, and ultimately still lose. The initial coverup was a rational decision, given Nixon's and his aides' belief that revelation of their complicity in the break-in would fatally damage his election chances. The coverup succeeded; the president won in a landslide. Ultimately, however, it was the coverup and not the "third-rate burglary" that brought him and his confederates down.

Nixon had a "fear of impotence."[14] To Nixon, the moment a leader shows timidity he encourages people to go after him.[15] Nixon must never show weakness; even being forthcoming is seen as "caving in."[16] The coverup took its form from Nixon's belief that nothing would be right unless he controlled the "way of it."[17] But Nixon, throughout the taped discussions Watergate, never judged the rightness of the "way" in terms of any criteria of ethics or morality. When Nixon pronounced in his March 21, 1973 conversation with Dean that it would be "wrong" to pay a million dollars to Hunt, he was referring to the practical problem of relating hush money to clemency. But the money had to be paid "damn soon."[18] The constant focus on current contingencies precluded consideration of long-range strategies. Nixon lurched from crisis to crisis.

Personality, however, is not determinative, it is a matter of tendencies. The essential fact of individual choice remains.

Nixon became deeply involved in the Watergate affair immediately after the June 17 arrests. On June 20 he and Haldeman discussed Watergate; the president apparently believed the conversation to be damning since the tape was later intentionally erased. On June 23, he ordered that the CIA shut off the FBI investigation.

He could have acted differently. He could have gone before the American people and "come clean" about the whole affair, admitted his culpability and dismissed those directly responsible. Even much later, he could have saved himself. For example, the president could have ended the Ervin committee inquiry early simply by appearing before it. "If the President had come to testify, he would have bowled the legs out from under [it]."[19] Once the existence of the White House taping system was revealed, he could have destroyed the tapes and, in the opinion of many, including Special Prosecutor Jaworski, would have gotten away with it. Jaworski believes that "despite the criticism such a desperate act would create . . . Nixon would have survived and remained in office."[20]

Past Decisions

With each succeeding "game" that Nixon played, his available effective strategies became increasingly limited. Each succeeding game was defined by the outcomes of those that preceded it. Once the president embarked on the coverup course certain decisions and courses of action (such as coming clean) were either closed[21] or had become increasingly costly. Furthermore, identical actions by Nixon at different times would have had profoundly different results. For example, Nixon's defiance of the unanimous Supreme Court in July 1974 would have led to his immediate impeachment and conviction. However, if Nixon had decided to appeal the first tapes case to the Supreme Court in October 1973, he probably would have faced a divided court.[22] The Supreme Court might have been reluctant to decide against the president since the *guarantee* of impeachment did not exist. By late spring and early summer 1974, the court was in a better position vis-à-vis the president. The House

Judiciary Committee had sat for months and it was likely that impeachment charges would be recommended by the committee and adopted by the House. Defiance of the court would have ensured his impeachment.

Information and Communication

The more complete the information a player has, the better he can take into account the possible actions of the other players. The Saturday Night Massacre game demonstrated the disastrous consequences of the president's lack of information about Richardson's preferences (if, indeed, Richardson had strict preferences prior to Cox's Saturday press conference). As we have seen, Nixon and Richardson had not spoken to each other all week; their first contact came when Richardson tendered his resignation. If Nixon had met with Richardson, he either would have been able to determine directly Richardson's preferences, or, if Richardson had none, a meeting might have compelled the attorney general to rank the outcomes *before* the president had forced a confrontation with Cox.

This failure to communicate had both personal and situational roots. One of the most salient elements of Nixon's style was his isolation.[23] Nixon relied on an extremely small group of intimates for information and advice. The removal of his two most trusted aides, Haldeman and Ehrlichman, simply meant the substitution of Haig and Zeigler.

Also, throughout the two weeks prior to the Saturday Night Massacre, Nixon was almost totally preoccupied with the Middle East war. Détente seemed to be collapsing and a direct collision between the United States and the Soviet Union seemed possible. On Friday October 19 and Saturday October 20 Nixon was heavily involved in the Middle East situation. Throughout this time, Nixon relied on Haig and others to deal with Richardson and Cox.

Rules of the Judicial Game

The Watergate tapes and the later writings of Nixon, Haldeman, Dean, and Magruder demonstrate that they saw all of government as essentially a public relations exercise. Their primary concern was image, not substance. Watergate was viewed as something to be overcome by "PR offensives," political manipulation, and rhetoric. In speech after speech, Nixon urged the public to forget the Watergate nonsense and move on to other concerns. Most of Nixon's former successes, from the "Checkers" speech on, resulted not from providing new facts but by giving new explanations, not by acting but by redefining the meaning of previous acts.[24] This strategy failed when he tried to deal with Watergate since the judiciary was immune to political and public relations pressures. Court proceedings focus attention on a specific set of experiences; briefs are filed, motions are made; evidence is presented; and verdicts are reached.

Once Watergate got into the courts, Richard Nixon's much-valued "options" were severely circumscribed. The risks were vastly more dangerous than in the looser arena of politics and public opinion. The judicial "rules of the game" are highly formalized, not subject to manipulation. Grand juries cannot be filibustered; they indict, and petit juries reach verdicts. Appeals are heard and decided. Defiance results in contempt citations.[25] Supreme Court justices do not brook political interference. But Richard Nixon never seemed to understand the nature of the legal "game." As late as March 1974, he was writing memos to Haig declaring that the "law case will be decided by the PR case."[26]

"Chance"

Much has been written that Nixon's fall demonstrated that our political/constitutional system "worked"—that existing structures and procedures were adequate to safeguard our freedom. This is only partially true. An important element in Richard Nixon's fall was the role of accident or "chance" (or at least factors not likely to be repeated). The extensive White House taping system installed by Nixon himself provided *the* evidence that brought the president and his aides down. Furthermore, the revelation of the taping system was essentially an accident. On July 13, 1973, at the end of a long afternoon of a long week, four Ervin Committee investigators "stayed just a little longer, asked one more question" of Alexander Butterfield, and uncovered the well-kept secret of the tape system.[27] (Even Ehrlichman was unaware of it.)

Without the tapes, "Watergate" would have been a conflict between the president of the United States and John Dean, a self-admitted criminal. There would have been no Saturday Night Massacre, no Supreme Court decision, no "smoking gun." Richard Nixon would have served his second term damaged but not destroyed.

There is also a "chance" element in "Maximum John" Sirica's presiding over the break-in trial. Sirica's highly unusual assumption of a prosecutorial role, and his imposition of extremely severe sentences, radically altered the game being played by the low-level conspirators. McCord's defection, and then Dean's and Magruder's, were rational responses to the changed decisional environment produced by Sirica.

In summary, Richard Nixon fell not because he was "mad" or "needed to fail" but because he and others made decisions to attain certain goals in situations of conflict and uncertainty. The interactions of these choices (and "chance") led to outcomes that were ultimately unfavorable to the president.

Notes

Introduction

1. Paul J. Halpern in the "Introduction" to his *Why Watergate?* provides an excellent discussion of the different levels of Watergate explanation and catalogs the various Watergate interpretations. Anyone interested in the "causes" of Watergate should begin with Halpern. The only drawback is that he wrote in 1975. Paul J. Halpern, ed., *Why Watergate?* (Pacific Palisades, California: Palisades Publishers, 1975), pp. 1–12.

2. Arthur Schlesinger, Jr., *The Imperial Presidency* (Boston: Houghton Mifflin Co., 1973).

3. Henry Steele Commager, "The Shame of the Republic," *New York Review of Books*, August 19, 1973, pp. 10–17.

4. Richard E. Neustadt, "The Constraining of the President," *New York Times Magazine*, October 14, 1973, p. 39.

5. Carl Oglesby, *The Yankee and Cowboy War: Conspiracies from Dallas to Watergate* (Kansas City: Sheed Andrews and McMeel, Inc., 1976).

6. Jonathan Schell, *The Time of Illusion* (New York: Alfred A. Knopf, 1976).

7. James Fallows, "Crazies by the Tail: Bay of Pigs, Diem and Liddy," *Washington Monthly*, September 1974, pp. 50–58.

8. Frank Fox and Stephen Parker, "Why Nixon Did Himself In: A Behavioral Examination of His Need to Fail," *New York,* September 9, 1974, pp. 26–32.

9. David Abrahamsen, *Nixon vs. Nixon: An Emotional Tragedy* (New York: Farrar, Straus and Giroux, 1977).

10. William Buckley, "Was Nixon Just Stupid?" *New York Post,* May 10, 1977, p. 30.

11. John Osborne, *The Fifth Year of the Nixon Watch* (New York: Liveright, 1974), p. 179.

12. Max Ways, "Watergate as a Case Study in Management," *Fortune*, November 1973, pp. 109–111.

13. Halpern discusses 30. There are dozens more.

14. Abraham Kaplan, *The Conduct of Inquiry: Methodology for Behavioral Science* (San Francisco: Chandler Publishing Co., 1964), p. 39.

15. Martin Shubik, "The Uses of Game Theory," in James C. Charlesworth, ed., *Contemporary Political Analysis* (New York: Free Press, 1967), p. 240.

16. John von Neumann and Oskar Morgenstern, *Theory of Games and Economic Behavior* (Princeton, N.J.: Princeton University Press, 1944).

17. Two recent compilations include several of the most relevant applications of game

theory. Peter Ordeshook, ed., *Game Theory and Political Science* (New York: New York University Press, 1978) and S.J. Brams, A. Schotter and G. Schwodiauer, eds., *Applied Game Theory* (Würzburg, West Germany: Physica-Verlag, 1979). Brams has extensively analyzed the Cuban missile crisis using several game-theoretic approaches. Steven Brams, *Game Theory and Politics* (New York: Free Press, 1975), pp. 39–47; *Paradoxes in Politics* (New York: Free Press, 1976), pp. 113–126; "Deception in 2 x 2 Games," *Journal of Peace Science*, Spring, 1977, pp. 189–194; "Nonmyopic Equilibria in Games and Politics: Foundations for a Dynamic Theory of Strategy," New York University, unpublished paper, 1976. Game theory has also been recently applied by John McDonald to historic American business decisions and by Brams to the Bible (Brams concludes that God is a superlative game player). John McDonald, *The Game of Business* (New York: Doubleday and Co., 1975). Steven Brams, *Biblical Games: A Strategic Analysis of Stories in the Old Testament* (Cambridge, Mass.: MIT Press, 1980). Brams' forementioned works include citations of game theory applications in political science.

18. Frank Zagare, "Deception in Three-person Games: An Analysis of Strategic Misrepresentation in Vietnam," Ph.D. dissertation, New York University, 1977; "A Game-Theoretic Analysis of the Vietnam Negotiations: Preferences and Strategies 1968–1973," *Journal of Conflict Resolution*, Vol. 21, December 1977, pp. 663–684; "The Geneva Conference of 1954: A Case of Tacit Deception," *International Studies Quarterly*, Vol. 23, September 1979, pp. 390–411.

19. McDonald, op. cit., p. xiv.

20. Karl Deutsch and Leroy N. Riesebach, "Empirical Theory," in Michael Haas and Henry S. Kariel, *Approaches to the Study of Political Science* (Scranton, Pa.: Chandler Publishing Co., 1970), p. 90.

21. Karl Deutsch, *The Nerves of Government: Models of Political Communication and Control* (New York: Free Press, 1966), p. 57.

22. McDonald, op. cit., p. 40. Formally, a strategy is a plan of action covering all contingencies. Theoretically, the complete explication of a strategy can be quite lengthy. Furthermore, the number of possible strategies can be extremely large. In reality, players simplify the content of strategies and limit the vast number of strategies open to them to the relatively few that they see as realistically worthwhile. The analyst limits the number of strategies to those he supposes the player actually considered (will actually consider).

23. *Ibid.*, p. xxv.

24. All works written by the Watergate principals must be assumed to be self-serving. Also, these works as well as the works of more detached observers are after-the-fact accounts and the authors may themselves be struggling to make sense of events. Given the obvious limits of relying exclusively on the public record, I believe that I have obtained "all" the relevant facts and have resolved conflicting accounts fairly.

25. In fact, the first two "games" are series of discrete but interrelated games.

26. J. Anthony Lukas, *Nightmare: The Underside of the Nixon Years* (New York: Viking Press, 1976), Chapter 9.

27. In a zero-sum game, the value ("payoff") of the game to all the players sums to zero. It is purely conflictual; what one player wins the other(s) must lose. In a nonzero-sum game, the sum of the payoffs is not equal to zero but varies according to the strategy choices of the players. Nonzero-sum games have both conflictual and cooperative dimensions; the players have mixed motives.

   For a discussion of Prisoner's Dilemma and Chicken, see Brams, *Game Theory*, pp. 30–47 and *Paradoxes*, Chapter 8; Anatol Rapaport and Albert Chammah, *Prisoner's Dilemma: A Study in Conflict and Cooperation* (Ann Arbor, University of Michigan

Press, 1965; and Nigel Howard, *Paradoxes of Rationality: Theory of Metagames and Political Behavior* (Cambridge: MIT Press, 1971), pp. 44–48, 176–177. 182–186.
    For discussions of deception-vulnerable games, see Zagare (footnote 18) and Brams (footnote 17). For an example, see the "Silbert Ploy," pp. 43–50. The single dilemma game is a one-sided variant of Prisoner's Dilemma. For an example, see the "Final Hunt-McCord" game, pp. 31–34.

28. The Ripon Society and Clifford W. Brown, *Jaws of Victory: The Game-Plan Politics of 1972, the Crisis of the Republican Party, and the Future of the Constitution* (Boston: Little Brown and Co., 1974), p. 11.

1. The Conspiracy Breakdown Games

1. Bernard Barker, Frank Sturgis, Virgilio Rodriguez, and Eugenio Martinez.

2. Hunt's name was found in two of the Cubans' address books by the FBI. He became the subject of a nationwide manhunt on July 1. On July 7, his attorney informed the FBI that Hunt would turn himself in. Liddy's name appeared in Martinez's address book. When FBI agents came to interview him, he refused to answer any questions and was summarily fired by Maurice Stans, the chairman of the Nixon campaign's finance committee.

3. For discussions of White House and election committee involvement with the Watergate break-in, see *The Senate Watergate Report: The Final Report of the Senate Select Committee on Presidential Campaign Activities* (New York: Dell Publishing Co., 1974), pp. 74–88 (henceforth, *Senate Watergate Report*) and *The Final Report of the Committee on the Judiciary, House of Representatives* (New York: Bantam Books, 1975), pp. 55–60 (henceforth, *Judiciary Committee Report*).

4. *Senate Watergate Report*, pp. 53–58.

5. *Ibid.*, p. 64.

6. *Ibid.*, p. 206.

7. *Ibid.*, p. 185.

8. *Ibid.*, p. 83. All these activities (except for the Huston Plan) involved a covert White House operation, the Special Investigations Unit. Since the unit was established to stop "leaks," its members were called the "Plumbers." The Watergate break-in was an outgrowth of the Plumbers' operation.

9. John Dean, *Blind Ambition: The White House Years* (New York: Simon and Schuster, 1976), p. 106.

10. *Ibid.*, p. 132.

11. Jeb Stuart Magruder, *An American Life: One Man's Road to Watergate* (New York: Pocket Books, 1974), p. 277.

12. Dean, op. cit., p. 124.

13. Dean, op. cit., p. 126.

14. Magruder, op. cit., p. 282.

15. Nixon notes the importance of Dean's monitoring of the FBI and grand jury investigations: "[it kept] us from being surprised by anything that emerged from them." Richard Nixon, *RN: The Memoirs of Richard Nixon* (New York: Grosset and Dunlap, 1978), p. 773. Dean had become the "linchpin" of the conspiracy. He was "the only one with the knowledge and personal rapport to reconcile the pitched camps at the White House and the Re-election Committee." Dean, op. cit., p. 125.

16. J. Anthony Lukas, *Nightmare: The Underside of the Nixon Years* (New York: Viking

Press, 1976), p. 247. For a highly critical look at Petersen, see Arthur Levine, "The Man Who Nailed Gordon Liddy," *Washington Monthly*, December 1974, pp. 38–48.

17. *Senate Watergate Report*, p. 105.

18. *Judiciary Committee Report*, p. 40.

19. *New York Times*, September 19, 1972, p. 1.

20. *Senate Watergate Report*, p. 108.

21. *Washington Post*, September 17, 1972, p. 1.

22. *The Presidential Transcripts* (New York: Dell Publishing Co., 1974), p. 36.

23. *Ibid.*

24. *Ibid.*, p.37.

25. *Ibid.*

26. Lukas, op. cit., p. 249.

27. George V. Higgins, *The Friends of Richard Nixon* (Boston: Little Brown and Co., 1975), p. 33.

28. *Ibid.*, p. 34. Higgins presents an excellent discussion of prosecutorial strategy which is drawn from below.

29. *Ibid.*, p. 32.

30. Samuel Dash, *Chief Counsel: Inside the Ervin Committee - The Untold Story of Watergate* (New York: Random House, 1976), p. 52.

31. G. Gordon Liddy, *Will* (New York: St. Martin's Press, 1980), p. 352.

32. Lukas, op. cit., p. 252.

33. "Mission Impossible: The Watergate Bunglers," an interview with Bernard Barker and Eugenio Martinez, *Harper's*, October 1974, p. 57.

34. Lukas, op. cit., p. 255.

35. *Senate Watergate Report*, p. 127. These and later promises of executive clemency were represented as being authorized by "high officials close to the President." They were. Nixon, *RN*, p. 645.

36. The Cubans' role is articulated by Bernard Barker: "I was not there at the Watergate to think. I was there to follow orders." William Lee Miller, "Some Notes on Watergate and America," *Yale Review*, March 1974, p. 321.

37. Liddy, op. cit., p. 353.

38. Late in the evening of May 27, 1972 the seven-member team broke into the Democratic National Committee (DNC) offices and placed electronic bugging devices on the telephones of two DNC officials. Papers from DNC files were photographed. However, there was a technical problem with one wiretap and the other had been improperly placed. These problems led to the fateful second break-in on June 17. Also, the Watergate conspirators unsucessfully attempted to bug George McGovern's Washington campaign headquarters on May 26 and May 28. For a more complete discussion of these episodes, see *Senate Watergate Report*, pp. 83–87.

39. For example, Colson, to Watergate and the forged Diem cables; Krogh, Young, and Ehrlichman to the Fielding break-in; Dean, for ordering him to flee the country after the burglars were apprehended.

40. "Probably" since he could have revealed Watergate involvement but not the other horrors and might have been rewarded accordingly.

41. Higgins, op. cit., p. 56.

42. Ordinal values indicate preference but do not account for the *intensity* of preference. For a justification of the use of ordinal versus cardinal utility, see Nigel Howard, *Paradoxes of Rationality: Theory of Metagames and Political Behavior* (Cambridge, Mass.: MIT Press, 1971), pp. xvii, 2.

43. Rational outcomes in two-person games are outcomes that result from the choice of dominant strategies by both players or the choice of a dominant strategy by one player and the choice of that strategy by the other player (who has no dominant strategy) which when intersected with the first's dominant strategy produces the higher outcome for the second. When neither player has a dominant strategy both choose their strategy that leads to an equilibrium outcome. Pareto superior equilibria are preferred to Pareto inferior equilibria. If there is no equilibrium there is no rational outcome. None of the games analyzed here lack an equilibrium. A dominant strategy is a strategy which leads to an outcome at least as favorable as any other strategy and, for at least one strategy of the opponent, leads to a better outcome than any other strategy. An outcome is in equilibrium if neither player gains by changing his strategy unilaterally.

   An example of a rational outcome resulting from the intersection of two dominant strategies is found in the "(Post-McCord) Dean-Magruder" game in Figure 1.6. Examples of a rational outcome resulting from the intersection of a dominant strategy and a strategy choice anticipating the choice of a dominant strategy are found in the "Final Hunt-McCord" game in Figure 1.3 (b), the Nixon-Sirica game in Figure 2.9 and the Nixon-Burger/Blackmun game in Figure 3.4. Examples of a rational outcome that is an equilibrium outcome are found in the "Initial Hunt-McCord" game in Figure 1.2; the "Actual Dean-Magruder Game After Dean Defection" in Figure 1.7.

   In the "Initial Hunt-McCord" game there are two equilibrium outcomes. Outcome A is Pareto optimal. There is no other outcome that enables both players to do better simultaneously. Outcome D is also in equilibrium but is inferior to outcome A. A single Pareto equilibrium is "prominent," as defined by Schelling. Thomas Schelling, *The Strategy of Conflict* (Cambridge: Harvard University Press, 1960), Chapters 1 and 2.

44. Lukas, op. cit., p. 249.

45. *Senate Watergate Report*, p. 139.

46. For an extensive discussion of the Patman episode, see Marjorie Boyd, "The Watergate Story: Why Congress Didn't Investigate Until After the Election," *Washington Monthly*, April 1973, pp. 37–45.

47. The Watergate issue apparently had little or no effect on the outcome. Indeed, an October Gallup poll found that 48 percent of the respondents had never *heard of* Watergate.

48. *Senate Watergate Report*, p. 117.

49. Lukas, op. cit., p. 258.

50. *Ibid.*, p. 261.

51. *Ibid.*, p. 262.

52. Dean, p. 173. According to Dean, Hunt was afraid that Judge Sirica would "stick him in jail forever" (p. 176).

53. Lukas, op. cit., p. 263.

54. In a January 8 telephone conversation Nixon outlined the clemency scenario to Colson: "I, uh, the question of clemency. . . . Hunt's is a simple case. I mean, after all, the man's wife is dead. . . . We'll build up that son-of-a-bitch like nobody's business." H. R. Haldeman, *The Ends of Power* (New York: Times Books, 1978), pp. 225–226.

55. Lukas, op. cit., p. 263.

56. Higgins, op. cit., pp. 33–34.

57. *Ibid.*, pp. 138–139. There is disagreement between Silbert and McCord's attorney, Gerald Alch, concerning the date of the second plea offer. Alch, in his testimony before the Ervin Committee in May 1973 stated that the offer was made in November 1972. Silbert, in March 1973, stated that the offer was made in January 1973 during the first week of the break-in trial. For excerpts of Alch's testimony, see the *New York Times*, May 24, 1973, pp. 32–33; for Silbert's statement, see the *Washington Post*, March 28, 1973, p. A10. The date of the second plea offer does not affect the analysis. However, the discrepancy between the versions of the two men directly involved is a good example of the difficulty in ascertaining the "facts" of Watergate.

58. McCord testimony before the Ervin Committee. *The Watergate Hearings: Break-in and Cover-up* (New York: Viking Press, 1973), p. 167.

59. Ibid.

60. Ibid., pp. 167–168.

61. Lukas, op. cit., p. 266.

62. *Senate Watergate Report*, p. 127.

63. Ibid., p. 128.

64. *Watergate Hearings*, p. 153.

65. Higgins, op. cit., pp. 135–136.

66. Ibid., p. 155.

67. John J. Sirica, *To Set the Record Straight: The Break-in, The Tapes, The Conspirators, The Pardon* (New York: W. W. Norton, 1979), p. 68.

68. *New York Times*, January 13, 1973, p. 1.

69. Lukas, op. cit., p. 269.

70. *Watergate and the White House: June 1972–July 1973*, Vol. I (New York: Facts on File, 1973), p. 20 (henceforth, *Facts on File*).

71. Dean testimony before the Ervin Committee. *Watergate Hearings:* pp. 282–283. The other members were Sam Ervin (D-South Carolina), Herman Talmadge (D-Georgia), Daniel Inouye (D-Hawaii), Joseph Montoya (D-New Mexico), Lowell Weicker (R-Connecticut) and Howard Baker (R-Tennessee).

72. *Transcripts*, p. 63.

73. Lukas, op. cit., p. 287. For an extensive discussion of the Gray confirmation hearings, see Barry Sussman, *The Great Cover-Up: Nixon and the Scandal of Watergate* (New York: New American Library, 1974), pp. 163–174.

74. *Facts on File*, p. 21

75. *Transcripts*, p. 96.

76. Lukas, op. cit., p. 293.

77. Ibid.

78. Ibid., p. 291.

79. Ibid.

80. *Transcripts*, p. 99.

81. Ibid., pp. 110, 114, 116.

82. Ibid., p. 110.

83. Ibid., p. 112.

84. Nixon, *RN*, p. 777.

85. Haldeman, op. cit., p. 238.

86. Ibid., p. 240.

87. Ibid.

88. Dean, op. cit., p. 241.

89. Ibid., pp. 194–195.

90. On March 20, Nixon told Haldeman, "Our real concern is Mitchell. . . . Maybe they're going to get him anyway." On March 21, Haldeman remarked, "I wonder if we are taking all this to protect John Mitchell." Lukas, op. cit., p. 300.

91. Sirica, op. cit., p. 95.

92. Ibid.

93. Ibid., p. 96.

94. *Facts on File*, p. 25.

95. Sirica, op. cit., p. 97.

96. Lukas, op. cit., p. 303; Sussman, op. cit., p. 178.

97. William Safire, *Before the Fall: An Inside View of the Pre-Watergate White House* (New York: Belmont Tower Books, 1975), p. 636.

98. Higgins, op. cit., p. 227.

99. Dash, op. cit., p. 36.

100. For excerpts of the *Times* story and for further statements by McCord, see *Facts on File*, p. 25.

101. For an extensive summary of Gray's testimony, see ibid., pp. 20–25.

102. *Transcripts*, p. 119.

103. *Facts on File*, p. 25.

104. Dean, op. cit., p. 214.

105. Higgins, op. cit., p. 173.

106. Dean, op. cit., pp. 188, 210–212.

107. Dean, op. cit., p. 219–220.

108. Ibid., p. 220.

109. Ibid., p. 221.

110. Magruder, op. cit., p. 339.

111. Ibid., p. 342.

112. Ibid., p. 343.

113. Ibid., pp. 343–344.

114. Dean, op. cit., p. 209.

115. Ibid., p. 213.

116. Magruder, op. cit., p. 348.

117. Ibid.

118. Higgins, op. cit., p. 166.

119. Richard Ben-Veniste and George Frampton, Jr., *Stonewall: The Real Story of the Watergate Prosecution* (New York: Simon and Schuster, 1977), p. 101.

120. Magruder, op. cit., p. 343.

121. Dean, op. cit., p. 245.

122. Steven Brams, "Deception in 2 x 2 Games," *Journal of Peace Science*, Spring, 1977, pp. 171–203.

123. Dean, op. cit., p. 235.

124. Ibid.

125. Ibid., p. 236.

126. Ibid.

127. Lukas, op. cit., p. 310.

128. Ibid., p. 307.

129. Ibid.

130. *Transcripts*, p. 233.

131. Lukas, op. cit., p. 313.

132. Nixon quoted in ibid.

133. Dean, op. cit., p. 248 (emphasis in original).

134. Lukas, op. cit., p. 317.

135. Dean, op. cit., p. 249.

136. Lukas, op. cit., p. 332.

137. Haldeman, op. cit., p. 257.

138. Dean, op. cit., p. 266.

139. Ibid.

140. *Transcripts*, p. 577.

141. *Facts on File*, p. 29.

142. Nixon, *RN*, p. 831.

143. Dean, op. cit., p. 160.

144. Haldeman, op. cit., p. 261.

145. Lukas, op. cit., p. 162.

146. Dean, op. cit., p. 270.

147. *Facts on File*, p. 30.

148. *Washington Post*, April 19, 1973 pp. A1, A12.

149. Dean, op. cit., p. 272.

150. Lukas, op. cit., p. 334.

151. *Facts on File*, pp. 37–38.

152. Higgins, op. cit., p. xiii.

2. The Saturday Night Massacre Game

1. On May 1, the Senate passed a resolution with wide bipartisan support calling on the president to appoint a special Watergate prosecutor. A similar resolution was introduced in the House by 18 Republicans. Calls for a special prosecutor also came from the president of the American Bar Association, a caucus of the 31 Democratic governors

meeting in Huron, Ohio, and consumer advocate Ralph Nader. Press demands came from all over the country, including the *New York Times, Washington Post, St. Louis Post-Dispatch, Virginia-Pilot* (Norfolk), *Courier-Journal* (Louisville).

2. Nixon wanted something less than an independent special prosecutor, as is shown in his April 15 conversation with Haldeman: "This is not to prosecute the case. A special prosecutor to look at the indictments, to see that the indictments run to everybody they need to run to. So that it isn't just the President's men, you see." *The Presidential Transcripts* (New York: Dell Publishing Co., 1974), p. 402.

3. For the text of the guidelines, see *Watergate: Chronology of a Crisis*, Vol. 1 (Washington, D.C.: Congressional Quarterly, 1973), p. 97. In November 1973 Judge Gerhard Gesell ruled that Cox's firing was illegal since it violated these regulations.

4. Ibid., p. 98.

5. Fred Thompson, *At That Point in Time* (New York: Quadrangle, 1975), p. 72.

6. James Doyle, *Not Above the Law* (New York: William Morrow, 1977), p. 94. Doyle was Cox's press secretary and presumably privy to his thinking.

7. *New York Times*, July 27, 1973, p. 1.

8. *Watergate: Chronology of a Crisis*, Vol. 2 (Washington, D.C.: Congressional Quarterly, 1974), p. 9.

9. Ibid., p. 16.

10. *Newsweek*, September 10, 1973, p. 19.

11. *Watergate: Chronology*, Vol. 2, p. 34.

12. J. Anthony Lukas, *Nightmare: The Underside of the Nixon Years* (New York: Viking Press, 1976), pp. 415–416.

13. *Watergate: Chronology*, Vol. 2, p. 34.

14. Ibid., p. 36.

15. For an extended discussion of the negotiations between the White House and Cox, see Doyle, op. cit., pp. 120–122.

16. For excerpts of their dissents, see *Watergate: Chronology*, Vol. 2, p. 59.

17. Ibid., p. 58.

18. Doyle, op. cit., p. 119.

19. *Presidential Transcripts*, p. 140.

20. Ibid., p. 133.

21. Bob Woodward and Carl Bernstein, *The Final Days* (New York: Simon and Schuster, 1976), p. 44.

22. For Laird's reaction, see *Congressional Quarterly: Weekly Report*, Vol. XXI, no. 42, October 20, 1973, p. 2779; for Griffin's, see David Broder, "Richardson, Cox Consult on Tapes, *Washington Post*, October 19, 1973, p. A1, A12; for Buckley's, see Frank Mankiewicz, *U. S. vs. Nixon*, (New York: Ballantine Books, 1975), pp. 111–112; for Brooke's, see *Washington Post*, September 14, 1973, p. A16; for Ervin's, see Clayton Fritchey, "Definitive Escape Clause," *Washington Post*, September 8, 1973, p. A15.

23. Elizabeth Drew, *Washington Journal: The Events of 1973–1974* (New York: Random House, 1975), p. 21. Such opinions were not universal. See John Connally's remarks in ibid. and Senator John Tower's in Mankiewicz, op. cit., p. 111.

24. Joseph Alsop, "The White House and the Courts," *Washington Post*, September 28, 1973, p. A29.

25. Roland Evans and Robert Novak, "Mr. Nixon: Determined to Defy Supreme Court?" *Washington Post*, October 17, 1973, p. A19.

26. Richard Nixon, *RN: The Memoirs of Richard Nixon* (New York: Grosset and Dunlap, 1978), p. 928.

27. For an extensive discussion of the Agnew affair, see Richard M. Cohen and Jules Witcover, *A Heartbeat Away: The Investigation and Resignation of Vice President Spiro T. Agnew* (New York: Viking Press, 1974).

28. Nixon, *RN*, p. 1005.

29. Ibid., p. 912.

30. John Osborne, *The Fifth Year of the Nixon Watch* (New York: Liveright, 1974), pp. 175–176.

31. According to William Safire, "the 'bold stroke' and the leapfrog technique were the essence of the Nixon way of working." William Safire, *Before the Fall: An Inside View of the Pre-Watergate White House* (New York: Belmont Tower Books, 1975), p. 10. Nixon's psychology, particularly his behavior in times of severe stress, is the subject of his own *Six Crises* (Garden City: Doubleday and Company, 1962). The following quotes from that book provide insights into Nixon's thinking about crises.

> In meeting any crisis in life, one must either fight or run away. But one must do something. Not knowing how to act or not being able to act tears your insides out (p. 152).
> It is the crisis itself, more than the merits of the engagement which rallies people to a leader. Moreover, when the leader handles the crisis with success, the public support he receives is even greater (pp. 230–231).
> Decisive action relieves the tension which builds up in a crisis (p. 131).

Nixon's absorption with the liberating effects of decisive action is seen in the White House anouncement of October 19. "What matters most, in this critical hour is our [read: my] ability to act—and to act in a way that enables us [read: me] to control events, not be paralyzed and overwhelmed by them." *Watergate: Chronology*, Vol. 2, p. 89.

32. Nixon, *RN*, p. 929. The "big play" was drawn from an article by constitutional scholar Alexander Bickel. Alexander Bickel, "The Tapes, Cox, Nixon," *The New Republic*, September 29, 1973, p. 13.

33. Elliot Richardson, "The Saturday Night Massacre," *Atlantic*, March 1976, p. 13.

34. Richardson, op. cit., p. 69.

35. According to Nixon, Richardson expressed confidence to Haig that Cox would agree to the compromise. Nixon, *RN*, p. 930.

36. For an extended discussion of the meeting between Cox and Richardson, see Doyle, op. cit., pp. 145–146.

37. Ibid., p. 49.

38. On October 7, Israel was attacked on two fronts. In the first four days, the Israelis lost one-fifth of their air force and a third of their armor. The Soviets were massively supplying the Arabs with their most sophisticated weapons. Israel's survival was endangered. By October 12, the Israelis counterattacked and had recaptured the Golan Heights; the situation on the Sinai remained critical. The United States began airlifting materiel on October 13. On Tuesday, October 16, Nixon "was directing the . . . greatest gamble of his diplomacy," risking a direct clash with the Soviets. Theodore H. White, *Breach of Faith: The Fall of Richard Nixon* (New York: Atheneum Publishers, 1973), pp. 260–261.

39. Aaron Latham, "Seven Days in October," *New York*, April 29, 1974. p. 45.

40. Doyle, op. cit., (p. 140) reports that on Tuesday, Richardson had included in his draft of the White House proposal a section, "Other Tapes and Documents," which provided for future judicial access by the special prosecutor. Buzhardt persuaded Richardson to remove the section for "stylistic" reasons. Since the Stennis compromise dealt only with the nine subpoenaed tapes, the inclusion of the section would be redundant. Subsequent events indicate that more than literary considerations were at issue.

41. Richard Ben-Veniste and George Frampton, Jr., *Stonewall: The Real Story of the Watergate Prosecution* (New York: Simon and Schuster, 1977), p. 128.

42. Ibid., p. 130.

43. Ibid., p. 131.

44. *Watergate: Chronology*, Vol. 2, pp. 90–91.

45. Woodward and Bernstein, op. cit., p. 64.

46. Latham, op. cit., pp. 41–58.

47. *Watergate: Chronology*, Vol. 2, p. 91.

48. Nixon, *RN*, p. 931.

49. Ibid., p. 929.

50. Osborne, op. cit., p. 176.

51. Alexander Haig, cited in *U. S. News and World Report*, November 5, 1973, p. 67.

52. Woodward and Bernstein, op. cit., p. 65.

53. Mankiewicz, op. cit., p. 14.

54. Woodward and Bernstein, op. cit., p. 64.

55. Doyle, op. cit., p. 183–184. Outcome G would have provided Richardson and Cox with the same payoffs as outcome C. However, Richardson's strategy that would have produced that outcome, "resign if Cox remains, remain if Cox resigns," is *dominated* by his "remain regardless" strategy. That is, if Cox resigns both of these strategies produce the highest payoff for Richardson. However, if Cox remains, Richardson's "remain regardless" strategy results in his next-best outcome while his "resign if Cox remains, remain if Cox resigns" results in his worst.

56. Nixon, *RN*, p. 931.

57. Ibid., Nixon's decision can be conceptualized as resulting from the choice of one of two possible strategies. He could present the proposal without a limitation on access or he could present the proposal with a limitation on access. With both of these strategies, Cox and Richardson had the same strategy choices as in Figure 2.1. The president concluded that whichever strategy he chose, Cox would resign and Richardson would remain. He chose to impose the prohibition since he felt it would guarantee Cox's exit and preclude any further release of taped material. Clearly, this was his most preferred outcome.

58. Woodward and Bernstein, op. cit., p. 65.

59. Doyle, op. cit., p. 165.

60. Nixon, *RN*, p. 1005.

61. Woodward and Bernstein, op. cit., p. 65.

62. *Watergate: Chronology*, Vol. 2, p. 91.

63. Woodward and Bernstein, op. cit., p. 65.

64. Ibid., p. 66.

65. Lukas, op. cit., p. 433.

66. Osborne, op. cit., p. 178.

67. *Newsweek*, November 5, 1973, p. 24. Ervin and Baker's motivations and goals in accepting the plan are open to speculation. Two days earlier, Judge Sirica had dismissed the Watergate Committee's suit to obtain certain tapes on the grounds that the court had no jurisdiction in a congressional civil suit. According to Woodward and Bernstein (p. 66), the Senators agreed to the proposal because it would be "better than nothing." The relationship between the Ervin committee and Cox was somewhat strained; Cox had attempted through the courts to close down the committee's public hearings. Senator Ervin offers a contrary version: he and Baker did not see the implications of their assent and were duped by the White House. He was led to believe that the committee would be receiving verbatim transcripts. Sam Ervin, "A Personal Account by Sam Ervin, Jr., of His Meeting with President Richard Nixon Regarding the Release of Transcripts of the White House Tapes," in Dash, op. cit., pp. 267–272. Baker disputes Ervin. He states that the word "summary" was used throughout the White House talk. Baker claims that he did not know of the restrictions on Cox but that "it wouldn't have made any difference" to him if he had known. *New York Times*, October 21, 1973, p. 43B.

68. *Watergate: Chronology*, Vol. 2, p. 58.

69. Presidential advisor Melvin Laird quoted in Lukas, op. cit., p. 434.

70. Ibid., p. 435.

71. Mankiewicz, op. cit., p. 38.

72. Woodward and Bernstein, op. cit., p. 68.

73. Theodore White, op. cit., p. 264 (emphasis in original).

74. Woodward and Bernstein, op. cit., p. 68 (emphasis mine).

75. *Watergate: Chronology*, Vol. 2, p. 89.

76. Woodward and Bernstein, op. cit., p. 68.

77. Ibid.

78. Ibid.

79. For these and other reactions, see *Washington Post*, October 20, 1973, pp. A1, A8.

80. Doyle, op. cit., p. 179.

81. *Newsweek*, November 5, 1973, p. 24.

82. Lukas, op. cit., p. 435; White, op. cit., p. 265.

83. White, op. cit., p. 265.

84. Ben-Veniste and Frampton, op. cit., p. 137. Much later, Cox, when asked how sure he had been of Richardson, replied that "I was always eighty-five percent sure." Doyle, op. cit., p. 110.

85. Drew, op. cit., p. 50.

86. Ben-Veniste and Frampton, op. cit., p. 137.

87. Drew, op. cit., pp. 50–51.

88. Richardson's Thursday night "Why I Must Resign" letter, reproduced in Lukas, op. cit., p. 430.

89. Nixon, *RN*, p. 933.

90. *U. S. News and World Report*, November 5, 1973, p. 65.

91. The game tree (extensive form), rather than the matrix (normal form) representation of the game is analyzed here for the sake of clarity. The normal form of a game is usually the simpler since it reduces the sequences of moves presented in the game tree into one

single decision: the choice of a strategy. Also, the existence of dominant strategies and equilibrium outcomes are more clearly seen when the game is in its normal form. However, when one is interested in analyzing the game *as* a sequence of moves, that is, when one wants to retain the discrete decisions in the strategic structure of the game, the game tree is the appropriate form.

92. "When Richardson arrived at the White House, Haig appealed to him to withhold his resignation at least until the Mideast crisis had been resolved." Nixon, *RN*, p. 934. Richardson replied to Haig, "What do you want me to do, write a letter of resignation, get it notarized to prove I wrote it today, and let it surface next week?" Woodward and Bernstein, op. cit., p. 69. Richardson concluded, "that would never be believed." Lukas, op. cit., p. 437.

93. Ruckelshaus news conference of October 23, reported in *Watergate: Chronology*, Vol. 2, p. 74.

94. An indication of why Bork obeyed Nixon's order to fire Cox can be found in Bork's *New Republic* article in which Bork defended Nixon against the "liberals." In that article he chastised the "intellectually bankrupt" tendency of liberals to see what Bork feels are "ideological problems in moral terms." Robert Bork, "Why I am for Nixon," *New Republic*, June 1, 1968, pp. 19–22.

95. Richardson, op. cit., p. 71. An *apparatchik* is a Soviet Communist party functionary.

96. *Ibid.*

97. *New York Times*, October 23, 1973, p. 33.

98. Among the reasons for the great uneasiness regarding impeachment were: (1) it would polarize the nation; (2) depict the Democrats as trying to undo the 1972 election; and (3) exceed the evidence adduced up to that time. R. W. Apple, "There Was a Cancer Growing on the Presidency . . ." *The Watergate Hearings: Break-In and Coverup* (New York: Viking Press, 1973), p. 21.

99. Barry Sussman, *The Great Cover-Up: Nixon and the Scandal of Watergate* (New York: New American Library, 1974), p. 274.

100. Ibid., p. 244.

101. Lukas, op. cit., p. 441.

102. Sussman, op. cit., p. 275.

103. Lukas, op. cit., p. 441.

104. "The Great Tapes Crisis," *Newsweek*, October 29, 1973, p. 30.

105. "It Looks Very Grim," *Newsweek*, November 5, 1973, p. 24.

106. Mankiewicz, op. cit., p. 51.

107. Ben-Veniste and Frampton, op. cit., p. 152.

108. "It Looks Very Grim," p. 24.

109. Richard Reeves, "Nixon and the Twilight Zone," *New York*, p. 44.

110. Sirica had been charged throughout his involvement with Watergate with overstepping his bounds. For example, at the time of the trial of the "Watergate Seven," he was criticized by Joseph Rauh, former chairman of the liberal Americans for Democratic Action, for espousing "an ends-justifying-means" philosophy. Chesterfield Smith, president of the American Bar Association, was "concerned" that Sirica was perverting the criminal sentencing procedure. Monroe Friedman, dean of Hofstra University Law School, stated that Sirica "deserves to be censured." Lukas, op. cit., p. 305.

111. Nixon, *RN*, p. 937.

112. Ibid.

113. John Sirica, *To Set the Record Straight: The Break-in, the Tapes, the Conspirators, the Pardon* (New York: W. W. Norton, 1979), pp. 167–180.

114. *New York Times*, October 24, 1973, p. 1.

115. Sirica, op. cit., p. 169.

116. Ibid., p. 179–180.

117. Ibid., p. 180.

118. Osborne, op. cit., p. 175.

119. Nixon, *RN*, p. 935.

120. However, even here Nixon's behavior can be viewed as rational. There is reason to believe that he was, indeed, personally preoccupied with the possibly catastrophic events in the Middle East.

121. Drew, op. cit., p. 65.

122. Richardson, op. cit., p. 71.

123. Nixon, *RN*, p. 935.

124. According to Anatol Rapaport, game theory "never questions the rationality of the goals pursued by the contending parties. . . ." Anatol Rapaport, *Two-Person Game Theory: The Essential Ideas* (Ann Arbor: University of Michigan Press, 1966), p. 213.

125. Woodward and Bernstein, op. cit., pp. 64–65.

126. It is the dominant theme of Richardson's public and private communications. See Richardson's October 20 letter to Nixon in *Watergate: Chronology*, Vol. 2, p. 86 and his October 23 news conference statement on pp. 86–87.

127. Mankiewicz, op. cit., pp. 39–40.

128. E. E. Schattschneider, *Semi-Sovereign People: A Realist's View of Democracy* (Hinsdale, Illinois: Dryden Press, 1960), Chapter 2.

129. Mankiewicz, op. cit., p. 38.

130. White, op. cit., p. 265.

131. Drew, op. cit., p. 49.

132. Ben-Veniste and Frampton, op. cit., p. 136.

133. White, op. cit., p. 269.

134. Mankiewicz, op. cit., p. 42.

135. Edward Weisband and Thomas Franck, *Resignation in Protest: Political and Ethical Choices Between Loyalty to Team and Loyalty to Conscience in American Public Life* (New York: Grossman Publishers, 1975).

136. Ibid., Chapter 1.

137. Ibid., Chapter 2.

138. Ibid., p. 15.

139. Ibid., p. 47.

140. *Watergate: Chronology*, Vol. 2, p. 86.

141. Ibid., pp. 87–88.

142. Ibid.

143. Ibid., pp. 86–87.

144. *U. S. News and World Report*, November 5, 1973, p. 65.

145. *New York Times*, October 24, 1973, p. 32.

146. Ibid., p. 33.

147. White, op. cit., p. 251.

148. Lukas, op. cit., pp. 418–419.

3. The White House Tapes Games

1. S2611 was cosponsored by 55 senators; 47 were Democrats and eight were Republicans. Eight of the 16 members of the Senate Judiciary Committee were among the sponsors. Both the Senate bill and the House's HR11401 provided for Judge Sirica to appoint the special prosecutor. For the major provisions of the Senate bill see *Watergate: Chronology of a Crisis*, Vol. 2 (Washington, D.C.: Congressional Quarterly, 1974), p. 94. On December 11, floor action on both bills was postponed (and never taken up) due to the growing confidence in Jaworski.

2. For the text of the news conference, see ibid., pp. 112–116.

3. J. Anthony Lukas, *Nightmare: The Underside of the Nixon Years* (New York: Viking Press, 1976), p. 446.

4. Ibid.

5. Richard Ben-Veniste and George Frampton, Jr., *Stonewall: The Real Story of the Watergate Prosecution* (New York: Simon and Schuster, 1977), p. 189.

6. According to Mankiewicz (p. 62) when "translated into human beings," this arrangement was "not such a good bargain." Frank Mankiewicz, *U.S. vs. Richard M. Nixon* (New York: Ballantine Books, 1975).

7. *Watergate: Chronology*, Vol. 2, p. 124.

8. All quoted in ibid., p. 121.

9. *Washington Post*, November 4, 1973, p. A21.

10. *Time*, November 12, 1973, pp. 21–22.

11. This "devil theory" was advanced by Haig on December 6 at a hearing before Judge Sirica.

12. *Watergate: Chronology*, Vol. 2, pp. 132, 168.

13. Ibid., p. 180.

14. Lukas, op. cit., p. 482.

15. Ibid.

16. Ibid., p. 465.

17. Ben-Veniste and Frampton, op. cit., p. 217.

18. Beginning in January 1974, impeachment and how to avoid it dominated the president's thinking and activity. See Richard Nixon, *RN: The Memoirs of Richard Nixon* (New York: Grosset and Dunlap, 1978), pp. 971–980.

19. Lukas, op. cit., p. 480.

20. *New York Times*, January 31, 1974, p. 20.

21. Lukas, op. cit., p. 482.

22. Ibid.

23. *Watergate: Chronology*, Vol. 2, p. 238.

24. For the indictments themselves, see the *New York Times*, March 2, 1974, p. 14.

25. Elizabeth Drew, *Washington Journal: The Events of 1973–1974* (New York: Random House, 1975), p. 157.

26. Ben-Veniste and Frampton, op. cit., p. 257.

27. James Doyle, *Not Above the Law: The Battles of Watergate Prosecutors Cox and Jaworski* (New York: William Morrow, 1977), p. 270.

28. Ben-Veniste and Frampton, op. cit., p. 227.

29. Ibid., p. 225.

30. Leon Jaworski, *The Right and the Power: The Prosecution of Watergate* (New York: Reader's Digest Press, 1976), p. 100.

31. Ben-Veniste and Frampton, op. cit., p. 232.

32. Jaworski ruled out any effort by the prosecutors to analyze or summarize the evidence. They had to appear to be scrupulously neutral, making no inferences or characterizations of the evidence or they would open themselves to White House attacks. The "road map" was a series of short statements setting forth indisputable facts, each of which were followed by a list of tapes or other evidence supporting the statement. If the House Judiciary Committee members followed the "map" carefully they would reach the same conclusion the prosecutors had: that Richard Nixon was involved in a criminal conspiracy to obstruct justice. For an extensive discussion of the "road map" and its rationale, see Leon Jaworski, op. cit., pp. 99–108.

33. *Watergate: Chronology*, Vol. 2, p. 284.

34. Ibid., p. 317.

35. Ben-Veniste and Frampton, op. cit., p. 269.

36. Nixon, *RN*, p. 975.

37. Lukas, op. cit., p. 485.

38. Ibid.

39. Ibid., p. 487.

40. All quoted in ibid., p. 491.

41. Ben-Veniste and Frampton, op. cit., p. 273.

42. Jaworski, op. cit., p. 136. Nixon had repeatedly stated publicly that the sole motive for involving the CIA had been national security. His June 23, 1972 conversation with Haldeman demonstrated that Nixon's motives were political, designed to cover up White House and CREP involvement in the Watergate break-in, its planning, and execution. It was the June 23 conversation with Haldeman that convinced Nixon to reject Jaworski's deal. Nixon, *RN*, p. 1000.

43. *New York Times*, May 21, 1974, p. 28.

44. Jaworski, op. cit., p. 146.

45. Bob Woodward and Carl Bernstein, *The Final Days* (New York: Simon and Schuster, 1976), p. 182.

46. Clark Mollenhoff, *Game Plan for Disaster: An Ombudsman's Report on the Nixon Years* (New York: W. W. Norton, 1976), p. 346. Delay, in the hope that the public would become sick of, bored with, Watergate was a basic White House strategy throughout the entire affair.

47. Woodward and Bernstein, op. cit., p. 183.

48. Bob Woodward and Scott Armstrong, *The Brethren: Inside the Supreme Court* (New York: Simon and Schuster, 1979), p. 291.

49. Ibid.

50. Jaworski, op. cit., p. 147.

51. The Supreme Court is the most secretive of all American institutions. It is virtually unheard of for a justice to reveal anything specific about the court's case work. The only such breach of secrecy on record occurred in 1857 when the thrust of the *Dred Scott* decision was leaked in advance by Justice Catron to President Buchanan. Henry Abraham, *The Judicial Process* (New York: Oxford University Press, 1975), p. 345. Law clerks, too, are sworn to secrecy. To say anything definite about the workings of the court in any specific case is therefore difficult. Reports on the tapes case are contradictory concerning Burger's and Blackmun's role. See, "A Very Definitive Decision," *Newsweek*, August 5, 1974, pp. 23–26; "A Unanimous No to Nixon," *Time*, August 5, 1974, p. 20, 25; *New York Times*, August 5, 1974, p. 18; "Man Proposes but the Court Disposes," *National Review*, August 16, 1974, p. 906; Nina Totenberg, "Behind the Marble, Beneath the Robes," *New York Times Magazine*, p. 15+; Woodward and Bernstein, op. cit., p. 262.

52. "A Very Definitive Decision," op. cit., p. 24.

53. Although votes for *certiorari* are secret, and the reasons for a decision on certiorari are "seldom, if ever, disclosed" (Abraham, op. cit., p. 179), Totenberg (op. cit., p. 58), reports that Justices Burger, Blackmun, and White all voted against granting the writ. White is not included with Burger and Blackmun as a player in the subsequent analysis because he is not a Nixon appointee and there is no evidence from reports of the predecision deliberations that he ever considered supporting the president. Instead, it seems reasonable to infer that White preferred that the case proceed through the usual judicial process (that is, go next to the Court of Appeals).

54. *New York Times*, July 1, 1974, p. 10; The data on case agreement were derived from the November issues of *Harvard Law Review*, vols. 85–89 (1971–1975).

55. Ibid.

56. *New York Times*, July 10, 1974, p. 1.

57. *Washington Post*, July 9, 1974, p. A14.

58. Woodward and Armstrong, op. cit., p. 308 (emphasis in original).

59. The expectation at the time of the decision was that the court would rule against the president. See "The Court's Hard Questions," *Newsweek*, July 22, 1974, p. 18; and "The United States v. Richard M. Nixon, President, et al.," *Time*, July 22, 1974, pp. 15–17. *Washington Post*, July 9, 1974, p. 19.

60. *New York Times*, July 10, 1974, p. 1.

61. Woodward and Bernstein, op. cit., p. 255.

62. Rowland Evans and Robert Novak, "Mr. Nixon's Supreme Court Strategy," *Washington Post*, June 12, 1974, p. A29.

63. For a discussion of *Brown*, see Richard Kluger, *Simple Justice: The History of Brown vs. Board of Education and Black America's Struggle for Equality* (New York: Alfred A. Knopf, 1976), Chapters 25 and 26. The day following the decision in *United States* v. *Nixon*, the Court reverted to the conservative-liberal split that characterized the Burger court. The court ruled 5–4 in the Detroit desegregation case.

64. Arthur Schlesinger, Jr., *The Imperial Presidency* (Boston: Houghton Mifflin Co., 1973), p. 256.

65. Robert Scigliano, *The Supreme Court and the Presidency* (New York: Free Press, 1971), Chapter 2.

66. "The United States v. Richard M. Nixon, President, et al.," p. 10.

67. *New York Times*, July 10, 1974, p. 22.

68. For an extended discussion of the Cherokee cases see Charles Warren, *The Supreme Court in United States History*, Vol. I (Boston: Little Brown and Co., 1924), pp. 729–779.

69. Robert Jackson, *The Supreme Court in the American System of Government* (Cambridge: Harvard University Press, 1962), p. 23. Jackson continued, "Public opinion . . . seems always to sustain the power of the Court, even against attack by popular executives even though the public more than once has repudiated particular decisions." Constitutional scholar Raoul Berger, a critic of the "Imperial Court" ascribes the power of the court to "the notion that the black-robed Justices are a priesthood to whom was given sole charge of arcane mysteries." Raoul Berger, "The Imperial Court," *New York Times Magazine*, October 9, 1977, p. 115.

70. D. Grier Stephenson, Jr., "'The Mild Magistracy of the Law': U.S. v. Richard Nixon," *Intellect*, February, 1975, p. 292.

71. *Washington Post*, July 25, 1974, Sec. A, p. 16. .

72. The United States v. Richard M. Nixon, President, et al.," op. cit., p. 10.

73. Frank Mankiewicz, *U.S. vs. Richard M. Nixon: The Final Crisis* (New York: Ballantine Books, 1975), p. 204.

74. This motif is best captured in the president's August 22, 1973 televised address to the nation. He stated:

> . . . people who do not accept the mandate of 1972, who do not want the strong America that I want to build, who do not want the foreign leadership that I want to give, who do not want to cut down the size of this government bureaucracy . . . people who do not want these things naturally would exploit any issue—if it weren't Watergate, anything else—in order to keep the President from doing his job. . . . I think they would prefer that I fail." Quoted in John Osborne, *The Fifth Year of the Nixon Watch* (New York: Liveright, 1974), p. 133.

75. Jaworski, op. cit., p. 164.

76. Lukas, op. cit., p. 510.

77. *The Final Report of the Committee on the Judiciary, House of Representatives* (New York: Bantam Books, 1975), pp. 481–482 (emphasis in original).

78. Lukas, op. cit., p. 519.

79. Lou Cannon, "The Last 17 Days of the Nixon Reign," *Washington Post*, September 9, 1974, Sec. A, p. 1.

80. Woodward and Bernstein, op. cit., p. 276.

81. *The End of a Presidency* (New York: Bantam Books, 1975), p. 324.

82. *New York Times*, July 25, 1974, p. 20.

83. But the special prosecutor would brook no delay. Two days later, on July 26, Jaworski appeared before Judge Sirica requesting expedited delivery. Judge Sirica, irritated by St. Clair's proposed delay and angered by the discovery that St. Clair had not even listened to the tapes himself, instructed St. Clair to begin delivery immediately. The first tapes were turned over on July 29 and additional ones on August 2. Among these tapes was the famous "smoking gun" tape of June 23, 1972.

84. For discussions of the importance of the majority-rule principle in the court, see John H. Clarke, "Judicial Power to Declare Legislation Unconstitutional," *American Bar Association Journal,* 9 (November, 1923), pp. 689–692; Thomas Norton, "The Supreme Court's Five to Four Decisions," *American Bar Association Journal,* 9 (July, 1923), pp. 417–420; Herbert G. Pillen, *Majority Rule in the Supreme Court* (Washington, D.C.: Georgetown University, 1924).

85. It can reasonably be argued that the president preferred to comply with a unanimous decision (C) than an indefinitive ruling that he had been threatening to ignore (A), hence (C,A). This reversal of the ranking of the two compliance outcomes leads to essentially the same results that are subsequently described, except that the equilibrium outcome becomes (3,3) rather than (3,2), and the paradoxical consequence discussed in Section 3.4 disappears.

86. Louis Kohlmeier, *"God Save This Honorable Court!,"* (New York: Charles Scribner's Sons, 1972), p. 85.

87. Powell, along with Burger and Blackmun, could have been included as the court player, but since he originally favored granting *certiorari*, it seems reasonable to suppose that his views more closely resembled those of the justices initially predisposed against the president. The *New York Times* (July 1, 1974, p. 10) reported that "Justice Powell demonstrated the highest level of independence within the Nixon Bloc." *Time* (July 22, 1974, p. 16) described Powell as "one of the least predictable of the eight and most flexible of the Nixon appointees." Wherever Powell best fits, his role is not material to our analysis of the game since his vote would not change the initial court majority, adverse to the president, to a minority.

88. This account was drawn from Lukas op. cit., p. 519. One of the more intriguing allegations concerning Burger's role in the case is provided by Charles Colson, who quotes President Nixon as stating, "I think we'll really win in the Supreme Court. Burger thinks this whole thing is a disgrace." Colson does not claim to know whether Nixon had spoken directly with Burger or whether the president had drawn a conclusion based on second-hand information. "Colson Lawyer Clarifies Statement on Burger," *Washington Post,* January 1, 1975, p. A4. According to the *New York Times* (January 15, 1975, p. 16), "The Supreme Court information officer, Barrett McGurn, denied that the Chief Justice had discussed the pending case with Mr. Nixon. . . . According to the NBC broadcast, 'a source close to Richard Nixon' also denied that any conversation between Mr. Nixon and Mr. Burger had occurred."

89. Lukas, op. cit., p. 519.

90. Nixon, *RN*, p. 1020.

91. Haldeman, op. cit., p. 310.

92. This section is taken from Steven Brams and Douglas Muzzio, "Unanimity in the Supreme Court: A Game-Theoretic Explanation of the Decision in the White House Tapes Case," *Public Choice,* Winter, 1977, pp. 67–83.

93. Interestingly, *no* outcomes in the Figure 3.2 matrix representation—neither those that yield payoffs (4,3) nor (3,2)—are in equilibrium, but this fact is not relevant to the present analysis because it has been already established that this representation does not depict the game that was played.

94. For a description and analysis of the Prisoner's Dilemma see Anatol Rapoport and Albert Chammah, *Prisoner's Dilemma* (Ann Arbor: University of Michigan Press, 1965) and Steven Brams, *Game Theory and Politics* (New York: Free Press, 1975). An outcome is nonPareto-optimal if there exists another outcome that is either better for one player and does not hurt the other or is better for both players (as is the case in the White House tapes game).

95. Nigel Howard, *Paradoxes of Rationality: Theory of Metagames and Political Behavior* (Cambridge: MIT Press, 1971).

96. Metagame theory "rationalizes" (4,3) as the equilibrium outcome in the White House tapes game by making Burger and Blackmun's dissent from the Supreme Court majority opinion contingent on Nixon's compliance with the court's decision, as described in the text. For an excellent, relatively nontechnical presentation of metagame theory and a critical evaluation concerning applications see Steven Brams, *Paradoxes in Politics* (New York: Free Press, 1976), Chapters 4, 5 and 6.

97. *New York Times*, July 25, 1974, p. 22.

98. Lukas, op. cit., p. 516

99. For the Republican impeachment strategy as articulated by Representative James Rhodes (R—Arizona), see the *New York Times*, July 7, 1974, p. 17.

100. *New York Times*, July 25, 1974, p. 1, 24.

101. *New York Times*, July 25, 1974, p. 1.

102. Steven Brams and Douglas Muzzio, "Game Theory and the White House Tapes Case," *Trial,*, May 1977, pp. 48–53; Steven Brams and Douglas Muzzio, "Unanimity in the Supreme Court: A Game-Theoretic Explanation of the Decision in the White House Tapes Case," *Public Choice*, Winter 1977, pp. 67–83.

103. Renata Adler's criticism is particularly sharp; she states that "[o]ne has to read every one of the authors' assertions, from the most trivial to the most momentous with the caveat 'if true.'" She provides examples of Woodward and Armstrong's procedural and substantive shortcomings. Renata Adler, review of the *The Brethren*, *New York Times Book Review*, December 16, 1979, p. 1. George Higgins also has doubts about the accuracy of what is reported. Higgins finds it hard to believe that on the basis of "third-hand" information Woodward and Armstrong can know what the justices "thought of the cases" and "what they said to each other . . . in conference where only justices are present" (p. 97). Higgins calls their approach "totem-pole hearsay" (p. 97). George Higgins, "The Brethren's Clerks," *Harper's*, April 1980, pp. 96–101.

104. Woodward and Armstrong, op. cit., p. 291.

105. Ibid., p. 292.

106. Ibid., p. 293.

107. Ibid., p. 292.

108. Ibid., p. 309.

109. Ibid., p. 310.

110. Ibid., p. 292.

111. Ibid., p. 310.

112. Ibid., p. 54.

113. Ibid., p. 286.

114. Ibid., p. 287.

115. Ibid., p. 323.

116. Ibid., p. 335.

117. Ibid., p. 323.

118. Ibid., pp. 314–346.

119. Ibid., p. 340.

120. Ibid., p. 341.

Conclusion

1. The framework for this section is drawn from Steven Brams, *Biblical Games: A Strategic Analysis of Stories in the Old Testament* (Cambridge: MIT Press, 1980), pp. 166–169.

2. This inference is based on the following statement by Richardson: "For two generations the . . . greatness of Presidents had been expressed in terms of a *zero-sum game* with the Congress and the Cabinet." Elliot Richardson, "The Saturday Night Massacre," *Atlantic*, March 1976, p. 42, (emphasis mine).

3. John McDonald, *The Game of Business* (New York: Doubleday and Co., 1975), p. xxviii.

4. David Rodhe and Harold Spaeth, *Supreme Court Decision Making* (San Francisco: W. H. Freemen, 1976), p. 105. See pp. 195–203 for their "threat" analysis.

5. That personality is an important shaper of behavior was expounded by Nixon in his *Six Crises*:

> Reaction and response is uniquely personal in the sense that it depends on what the individual brings to bear on the situation—his own traits of personality and character, his training, his moral and religious background, his strengths and weaknesses.

Richard Nixon, *Six Crises* (Garden City, N.Y. Doubleday and Co, 1962), p. xxv.

6. Throughout his public career Nixon has been the subject of several psychohistorical and psychobiographical studies. The best known studies are: Bruce Mazlish, *In Search of Nixon: A Psychohistorical Inquiry* (Baltimore: Penguin Books, 1972); Eli Chesen, *President Nixon's Psychiatric Profile: A Psychodynamic-Genetic Interpretation* (New York: Peter H. Wyden, 1973); David Abrahamsen, *Nixon vs. Nixon: An Emotional Tragedy* (New York: Farrar, Straus and Giroux, 1977); and James David Barber, *The Presidential Character: Predicting Performance in the White House* (Englewood Cliffs, N.J.: Prentice-Hall, 1977). (Barber's study includes all presidents since Theodore Roosevelt.) Each of these works has been criticized. For criticism of Chesen, see Edwin Diamond, "Nixon and the Psychohistorians," *New York*, February 25, 1974, pp. 5–7. For Abrahamsen, see Robert S. Liebert, "Nixon and the Enemy Within," *Psychology Today*, March 1977, pp. 68–69. For Barber, see Alexander L. George, "Assessing Presidential Character," *World Politics*, Vol. 26, January 1974, pp. 234–282, and James Qualls, "Barber's Typological Analysis of Political Leaders," *American Political Science Review*, Vol. 71, March 1977, pp. 182–211. (See Barber's trenchant reply, "Comment: Quall's Nonsensical Analysis of Nonexistent Works," in the same issue, pp. 212–225.) For Mazlish, see Arnold Rogow's review in *Political Science Quarterly*, Vol. 87, December 1972, pp. 675–676. Barber's work is by far the most rigorous and most clearly related to Watergate; hence, the reliance on his work below.

7. Barber, op. cit., p. 13.

8. Ibid., p. 361.

9. Ibid., p. 395.

10. The Ripon Society and Clifford W. Brown, *Jaws of Victory: The Game-Plan Politics of 1972, the Crisis of the Repulican Party and the Future of the Constitution* (Boston: Little Brown and Co., 1974), p. 15. For a more complete discussion of the issues discussed below, see Chapters 1 and 5.

11. Ibid., p. 92.

12. Barber, op. cit., p. 386.

13. Ibid., p. 37

14. Jonathan Schell, *The Time of Illusion* (New York: Alfred A. Knopf, 1976), p. 373.

15. Barber, op. cit., p. 479.

16. Elizabeth Drew, *Washington Journal: The Events of 1973–1974* (New York: Random House, 1975), p. 198; J. Anthony Lukas, *Nightmare: The Underside of the Nixon Years* (New York: Viking Press, 1976), p. 338; and Theodore White, *Breach of Faith: The Fall of Richard Nixon* (New York: Atheneum Publishers, 1975), p. 294.

17. Lukas, op. cit., p. 326.

18. *The Presidential Transcripts* (New York: Dell Publishing Co., 1974), p. 112.

19. Terry Lenzer, a counsel to the Ervin committee, quoted in Barber, op. cit., p. 475.

20. Quoted in David Alpern, "Watergate: Jaworski Remembers," *Newsweek*, September 6, 1976, p. 17

21. The foreclosing of options was graphically explicated by Haldeman in an April 1973 conversation with Dean: "Once the toothpaste is out of the tube, it's going to be very hard to get it back in." Testimony by John Dean before the Senate Watergate Committee, *The Watergate Hearings: Break-in and Cover-up* (New York: Viking Press, 1973), p. 294.

22. Woodward and Armstrong state that Justice Brennan believed that the court was then split 4–4 over the issue of Nixon's claim of executive privilege with Justice White holding the decisive vote. Bob Woodward and Scott Armstrong, *The Brethren: Inside the Supreme Court* (New York: Simon and Schuster, 1979), p. 289.

23. Bruce Mazlish, "Nixon's Performance," *Washington Post*, November 26, 1973, p. A20.

24. Barber, op. cit., p. 475

25. For discussions of the impact of the rules of the judicial game, see Barber, op. cit., p. 475; Ripon and Brown, op. cit., pp. 112–113; and Frank Mankiewicz, *U.S. vs. Richard M. Nixon: The Final Crisis* (New York: Ballantine Books, 1975), pp. 2–4.

26. Richard Nixon, *RN: The Memoirs of Richard Nixon* (New York: Grossett and Dunlap, 1978), p. 990.

27. Barber, op. cit., p. 481. According to Sam Ervin, "In a very real sense the discovery [of the tapes] was fortuitous." Sam J. Ervin, *The Whole Truth-The Watergate Conspiracy* (New York: Random House, 1980), p. 186.

Bibliography

A. *Substantive Books*

Abraham, Henry. *The Judicial Process*. 3rd ed. New York: Oxford University Press, 1975.

Abrahamsen, David M.D. *Nixon vs. Nixon: An Emotional Tragedy*. New York: Farrar, Straus and Giroux, 1977.

Anderson, Jack. *The Anderson Papers*. New York: Random House, 1973.

Barber, James David. *The Presidential Character: Predicting Performance in the White House*. Englewood Cliffs, N.J.: Prentice-Hall, Inc., 1977.

Ben-Veniste, Richard, and Frampton, George, Jr. *Stonewall: The Real Story of the Watergate Prosecution*. New York: Simon and Schuster, 1977.

Block, Herbert. *Herblock Special Report*. New York: W. W. Norton and Co., 1974.

Breslin, Jimmy. *How the Good Guys Finally Won: Notes from an Impeachment Summer*. New York: Viking Press, 1975.

Buckley, William F. *Execution Eve and Other Contemporary Ballads*. New York: G. Putnam's Sons, 1975.

Chesen, Eli, M.D. *President Nixon's Psychiatric Profile: A Psychodynamic-Genetic Interpretation*. New York: Peter H. Wyden, 1973.

Chester, Lewis, McCrystal, Cal, Aris, Stephen, and Shawcross, William. *Watergate: The Full Story*. New York: Ballantine Books, 1973.

Cohen, Richard M., and Witcover, Jules. *A Heartbeat Away: The Investigation and Resignation of Vice President Spiro T. Agnew*. New York: Viking Press, 1974.

Cox, Archibald. *The Role of the Supreme Court in American Government*. New York: Oxford University Press, 1976.

Dash, Samuel. *Chief Counsel: Inside the Ervin Committee—The Untold Story of Watergate*. New York: Random House, 1976.

Dean, John. *Blind Ambition: The White House Years*. New York: Simon and Schuster, 1976.

Dean, Maureen. *"Mo": A Woman's View of Watergate*. New York: Simon and Schuster, 1975.

Doyle, James. *Not Above The Law: The Battles of Watergate Prosecutors Cox and Jaworski*. New York: William Morrow, 1977.

Drew, Elizabeth. *Washington Journal: The Events of 1973–1974*. New York: Random House, 1975.

The End of a Presidency. New York: Bantam Books, 1975.

Ervin, Sam J. *The Whole Truth-The Watergate Conspiracy.* New York: Random House, 1980.

Fields, Howard. *High Crimes and Misdemeanors: The Dramatic Story of the Rodino Committee.* New York: W. W. Norton and Co., 1978.

Frost, David. *"I Gave Them a Sword": Behind the Scenes of the Nixon Interviews.* New York: Ballantine Books. 1978.

Haldeman, H. R. *The Ends of Power.* New York: Times Books, 1978.

Halpern, Paul, ed. *Why Watergate?* Pacific Palisades, Cal.: Palisades Publishers, 1975.

Hamilton, Alexander, Madison, James, and Jay, John. *The Federalist Papers.* New York: New American Library, 1961.

Herbers, John. *No Thank You, Mr. President.* New York: W. W. Norton and Co., 1976.

Higgins, George V. *The Friends of Richard Nixon.* Boston: Little, Brown and Co., 1975.

Hunt, Howard. *Under-Cover: Memoirs of an American Secret Agent.* New York: Berkley Publishing Corp., 1974.

Impeachment of Richard M. Nixon, President of the United States. Report of the Committee on the Judiciary, U.S. House of Representatives. New York: Bantam Books, 1975.

Jackson, Robert H. *The Supreme Court in the American System of Government.* Cambridge: Harvard University Press, 1962.

Jaworski, Leon. *The Right and the Power: The Prosecution of Watergate.* New York: Reader's Digest Press, 1976.

Kluger, Richard. *Simple Justice: The History of Brown vs. Board of Education and Black America's Struggle for Equality.* New York: Alfred A. Knopf, 1976.

Kohlmeier, Louis M. *"God Save This Honorable Court!"* New York: Charles Scribner's Sons, 1972.

Liddy, G. Gordon. *Will.* New York: Dell/St. Martin's Press, 1980.

Lukas, J. Anthony. *Nightmare: The Underside of the Nixon Years.* New York: Viking Press, 1976.

Lurie, Leonard. *The Impeachment of Richard Nixon.* New York: Berkley Publishing Co., 1973.

McCarthy, Mary. *The Mask of State: Watergate Portraits.* New York. Harcourt Brace Jovanovich, 1973.

McCord, James: *A Piece of Tape: The Watergate Story Fact and Fiction.* Rockville, Maryland: Washington Media Services, 1974.

Magruder, Jeb Stuart. *An American Life: One Man's Road to Watergate.* New York: Pocket Books, 1974.

Mankiewicz, Frank. *Perfectly Clear: Nixon from Whittier to Watergate.* New York: Popular Library, 1973.

Mankiewicz, Frank. *U.S. vs. Richard M. Nixon: The Final Crisis.* New York: Ballantine Books, 1975.

Mazlish, Bruce. *In Search of Nixon: A Psychohistorical Inquiry.* Baltimore, Md.: Penguin Books, 1972.

Mezvinsky, Edward. *A Term to Remember.* New York: Coward, McCann and Geoghegan, 1977.

Mollenhoff, Clark R. *Game Plan for Disaster: An Ombudsman's Report on the Nixon years.* New York: W. W. Norton and Co., 1976.

Mosher, Frederick. *Watergate: Implications for Responsible Government.* New York: Basic Books, 1974.

Murphy, Walter. *Elements of Judicial Strategy.* Chicago: University of Chicago Press, 1964.

Nathan, Richard. *The Plot that Failed: Nixon and the Administrative Presidency.* New York: John Wiley and Sons, 1975.

Neustadt, Richard. *Presidential Power: The Politics of Leadership, With Reflections on Johnson and Nixon.* New York: John Wiley and Sons, 1976.

Nixon, Richard. *RN: The Memoirs of Richard Nixon.* New York: Grosset and Dunlap, 1978.

Nixon, Richard. *Six Crises.* Garden City, N.Y.: Doubleday and Co., 1962.

Oglesby, Carl. *The Yankee and Cowboy War: Conspiracies from Dallas to Watergate.* Kansas City: Sheed Andrews and McMeel, 1976.

Osborne, John. *The Fifth Year of the Nixon Watch.* New York: Liveright, 1974.

Osborne, John. *The Last Nixon Watch.* Washington, D.C.: New Republic Book Co., 1975.

Pillen, Herbert G. *Majority Rule in the Supreme Court.* Washington, D.C.; Georgetown University, 1924.

Powers, Thomas. *The Man Who Kept the Secrets: Richard Helms and the CIA.* New York: Alfred A. Knopf, 1979.

The Presidential Transcripts. New York: Dell Publishing Co., 1974.

Price, Raymond. *With Nixon.* New York: Viking Press, 1977.

Rather, Dan, and Gates, Gary Paul. *The Palace Guard.* New York: Warner Books, 1975.

Richardson, Elliot. *The Creative Balance: Government, Politics, and the Individual in America's Third Century.* New York: Holt, Rinehart and Winston, 1976.

The Ripon Society, and Brown, Clifford W. *Jaws of Victory: The Game-Plan Politics of 1972, the Crisis of the Republican Party and the Future of the Constitution.* Boston: Little Brown and Co., 1974.

Rodhe David, and Spaeth, Harold J. *Supreme Court Decision Making.* San Francisco: W. H. Freeman and Co., 1976.

Safire, William. *Before the Fall: An Inside View of the Pre-Watergate White House.* New York: Belmont Tower Books, 1975.

Schattschneider, E. E. *The Semi-Sovereign People: A Realist's View of Democracy in America.* New York: Holt, Rinehart and Winston, 1960.

Schell, Jonathan. *The Time of Illusion.* New York: Alfred A. Knopf, 1976.

Schelling, Thomas. *The Strategy of Conflict.* New York: Oxford University Press, 1960.

Schlesinger, Arthur, Jr. *The Age of Roosevelt: The Politics of Upheaval*. Boston: Houghton Mifflin Co., 1960.
Schlesinger, Arthur, Jr. *The Imperial Presidency*. Boston: Houghton Mifflin Co., 1973.
Scigliano, Robert. *The Supreme Court and the Presidency*. New York: Free Press, 1971.
The Senate Watergate Report: The Final Report of the Senate Select Committee on Presidential Campaign Activities. New York: Dell Publishing Co., 1974.
Sirica, John J. *To Set the Record Straight: The Break-in, The Tapes, The Conspirators, The Pardon*. New York: W. W. Norton, 1979.
Sorenson, Theodore. *Watchmen in the Night: Presidential Accountability After Watergate*. Cambridge, Mass.: MIT Press, 1975.
Sussman, Barry. *The Great Cover-Up: Nixon and the Scandal of Watergate*. New York: New American Library, 1974.
Szulc, Tad. *Compulsive Spy: The Strange Career of E. Howard Hunt*. New York: Viking Press, 1974.
Thompson, Fred D. *At That Point in Time: The Inside Story of the Senate Watergate Committee*. New York: New York Times Book Co., 1975.
Thompson, Hunter S. *The Great Shark Hunt: Strange Tales from a Strange Time*. New York: Summit Books, 1979.
von Hoffman, Nicholas. *Make-Believe Presidents: Illusions of Power from McKinley to Carter*. New York: Pantheon Books, 1978.
Warren, Charles. *The Supreme Court in United States History*. Vol. I. Boston: Little Brown and Co., 1924.
Watergate: Chronology of a Crisis. Vols. 1 and 2. Washington, D.C.: Congressional Quarterly, 1974.
Watergate and the White House: June 1972–July 1973. Vol. I. New York: Facts on File, 1973.
The Watergate Hearings: Break-in and Cover-up. New York: Viking Press, 1973.
Weisband, Edward, and Franck, Thomas. *Resignation in Protest: Political and Ethical Choices between Loyalty to Team and Loyalty to Conscience in American Public Life*. New York: Grossman Publishers, 1975.
Weismann, Steve. *Big Brother and the Holding Company: The World Behind Watergate*. Palo Alto, Cal.: Ramparts Press, 1974.
White, Theodore H. *Breach of Faith: The Fall of Richard Nixon*. New York: Atheneum Publishers, 1975.
White, Theodore H. *The Making of the President 1972*. New York: Atheneum Publishers, 1973.
Wills, Garry. *Nixon Agonistes: The Crisis of the Self-Made Man*. Boston: Houghton Mifflin, 1970.
Woodward, Bob and Armstrong, Scott. *The Brethren: Inside the Supreme Court*. New York: Simon and Schuster, 1979.
Woodward, Bob, and Bernstein, Carl. *All the President's Men*. New York: Warner Books, 1975.

Woodward, Bob, and Bernstein, Carl. *The Final Days*. New York: Simon and Schuster, 1976.

B. *Substantive Articles*

"About This Issue," *Harper's*, October 1974, pp. 4–5.

Adler, Renata. Review of *The Brethren: Inside the Supreme Court*, by Bob Woodward and Scott Armstrong, in the *New York Times Book Review*, December 16, 1979, p. 1.

Adler, Renata. "Searching for the Real Nixon Scandal: A Last Inference," *Atlantic Monthly*, December 1976, pp. 76–95.

Alpern, David. "Watergate: Jaworski Remembers," *Newsweek*, September 6, 1976.

Anderson, Jack. "Burger Readies for Date with Destiny," *Washington Post*, June 24, 1974, p. D15.

Anderson, Jack. "Nixon Seen Deeply Suspicious of Cox," *Washington Post*, October 25, 1973, p. G7.

Barber, James David. "Character Trap: President Nixon and Richard Nixon," *Psychology Today*, October 1974, pp. 113–118.

Barber, James David. "The Nixon Brush with Tyranny," *Political Science Quarterly*, Vol 92 (Winter 1977–1978), pp. 581–597.

Barber, James David. "Comment: Quall's Nonsensical Analysis of Nonexistent Works," *American Political Science Review*, Vol. 71 (March 1977), pp. 212–225.

"Behind the Eight Ball," *New Republic*, August 10 and 17, 1974, pp. 8–9.

Bensman, Joseph. "Watergate: In the Corporate Style," *Dissent,* Summer 1973, pp. 279–280.

Berger, Raoul, "The Imperial Court," *New York Times Magazine*, October 9, 1977, pp. 38, 39, 106, 110–118.

Bernstein, Barton J. "The Road to Watergate and Beyond: The Growth and Abuse of Executive Authority Since 1940," *Law and Contemporary Problems*, Spring 1976, pp. 58–86.

Bickel, Alexander. "The Tapes, Cox, Nixon," *New Republic*. September 29, 1973, pp. 13–14.

Bickel, Alexander. "Watergate and the Legal Order," *Commentary*, January 1974, pp. 19–25.

Bork, Robert. "Why I Am for Nixon," *New Republic*, June 1, 1968, pp. 19–22.

Boyd, Marjorie. "The Watergate Story: Why Congress Didn't Investigate Until After the Election," *Washington Monthly,* April 1973, pp. 37–45.

Branch, Taylor. "Crimes of Weakness," *Harper's*, October 1974, pp. 40–43.

Branch, Taylor. "Gagging on Deep Throat," *Esquire*, November 1976, pp. 10, 12, 62.

Buckley, William F. "Was Nixon Just Stupid?" *New York Post,* May 10, 1977, p. 30.

Burns, James MacGregor. Review of *RN: The Memoirs of Richard Nixon*, in the *New York Times Book Review*, July 11, 1978, p. 1 + .

Cannon, Lou. "The Last 17 Days of the Nixon Reign," *Washington Post*, September 29, 1974, p. A10.

Clarke, John H. "Judicial Power to Declare Legislation Unconstitutional," *American Bar Association Journal*, Vol. 9 (November 1923), pp. 689–692.

Clemons, Walter. "Dean's Story: A Rat's Nest," *Newsweek*, October 18, 1976, p. 29.

Commager, Henry Steele. "The Shame of the Republic," *New York Review of Books*, August 19, 1973, pp. 10–17.

Copeland, Miles. "The Unmentionable Uses of the C.I.A.," *National Review*, September 14, 1973, pp. 990–997.

Cox, Archibald. "Reflections on a Firestorm," *Saturday Review World*, March 9, 1974, pp. 12–14.

Diamond, Edwin. "Nixon and the Psychohistorians," *New York*, February 25, 1974, pp. 5–7.

Epstein, Edward Jay. "Did the Press Uncover Watergate?" *Commentary*, July 1974, pp. 21–24.

Etzioni, Amitai. "After Watergate—What? A Social Science Perspective," *Human Behavior*, November 1973, pp. 7–8.

Evans, Roland, and Novak, Robert. "Mr. Nixon: Determined to Defy the Supreme Court?" *Washington Post*, October 17, 1973, p. A19.

Evans, Roland, and Novak, Robert. "Resignation, Accusation and Confusion," *Washington Post*, November 17, 1973, p. A22.

Evans, Roland, and Novak, Robert. "A Unanimous Court Against Mr. Nixon?" *Washington Post*, June 23, 1973, p. C7.

Fallows, James. "Crazies by the Tail: Bay of Pigs, Diem and Liddy," *Washington Monthly*, September 1974, pp. 50–58.

Fox, Frank, and Parker, Stephen, "Why Nixon Did Himself In: A Behavioral Examination of His Need to Fail," *New York*, September 9, 1974, p. 26 + .

Fritchey, Clayton. "'Definitive' Escape Clause," *Washington Post*, September 8, 1973, p. A15.

Fuller, T. "St. Clair Speaks," *Newsweek*, October 25, 1976, p. 40.

Galbraith, John Kenneth. "The Good Old Days," review of *RN: The Memoirs of Richard Nixon*, in the *New York Review of Books*, June 29, 1978, p. 3.

Gelb, Leslie. "The Secretary of State Sweepstakes," *New York Times Magazine*, May 23, 1976, p. 13 + .

George, Alexander L. "Assessing Presidential Character," review of *The Presidential Character: Predicting Performance in the White House* by James David Barber in *World Politics*, Vol. 26 (January 1974), pp. 234–282.

Goodman, Walter. Review of *It Didn't Start With Watergate* by Victor Lasky, in the *New York Times Book Review*, May 8, 1977, pp. 7, 40.

Gorey, Hays. "Dean's Dilemma," *Harper's*, October 1974, pp. 63–65.

"The Great Tapes Crisis," *Newsweek*, October 29, 1973, pp. 22–30.

"Haig: 'Events that Led to the Fire Storm'," *U.S. News and World Report*, November 5, 1973, pp. 66, 69.

Hersh, Seymour. Review of *The Right and the Power: The Prosecution of*

Watergate, by Leon Jaworski, in the *New York Times Book Review*, September 19, 1976, pp. 2–3.

Higgins, George V. "The Brethren's Clerks," *Harper's*, April 1980, pp. 96–101.

Hougan, Jim. "The McCord File," *Harper's*, January 1980, pp. 37–56.

Howe, Irving. "Watergate: The Z Connection," *Dissent*, Summer 1973, pp. 275–278.

"How Good a Case?" *Newsweek*, July 29, 1974, pp. 16–29.

Hughes, Emmet John. "A White House Taped," *New York Times Magazine*, June 9, 1974, p. 17+.

"Impeachment and the Courts," *Nation*, June 8, 1974, p. 706.

"It Looks Very Grim," *Newsweek*, November 5, 1973, pp. 21–25.

Kempton, Murray. "Treason of the Clerks," *New York*, February 25, 1980, pp. 70–71.

Kohn, Howard. "Strange Bedfellows: The Hughes-Nixon-Lansky Connection: The Secret Alliances of the CIA from World War II to Watergate," *Rolling Stone*, May 20, 1976, pp. 39–92.

Kraft, Joseph. "It Will Get Worse Before It Gets Worse," *New York*, February 4, 1974, pp. 27–28.

Kraft, Joseph. "Maneuvering with the Tapes," *Washington Post*, October 21, 1973, p. C7.

Kraft, Joseph. "Now It's Up to the Court," *Washington Post*, July 9, 1974, p. A19.

Kraft, Joseph. "Watergate: Still a Live Issue," *Washington Post*, September 18, 1973, p. A21.

Kraft, Joseph. "Why Nixon Was Afraid of Archibald Cox," *New York*, November 5, 1973, pp. 39.

Lardner, George. "Behind the Scenes at the Cox Investigation," *Ramparts*, January 1974, pp. 21–26.

Lasch, Christopher. Review of *Nightmare: The Underside of the Nixon Years*, by J. Anthony Lukas, in the *New York Times Book Review*, January 25, 1976, pp. 23–24.

Latham, Aaron. "Seven Days in October," *New York*, April 29, 1974, pp. 41–57.

Lerner, Max. "Writing 'Hot History,'" *Saturday Review*, May 29, 1976, pp. 16–19.

Levine, Arthur. "The Man Who Nailed Gordon Liddy," *Washington Monthly*, December 1974, pp. 38–48.

Lewis, Anthony. "United States v. Nixon," *New York Times*, July 25, 1974, p. 33.

Liebert, Robert. "Nixon and the Enemy Within," review of *Nixon vs. Nixon: An Emotional Tragedy*, by David Abrahamsen, in *Psychology Today*, March 1977, pp. 68–69.

Lipset, Seymour Martin, and Raab, Earl. "Watergate: The Vacillation of the President," *Psychology Today*, November 1973, pp. 77–84.

Lukas, J. Anthony. Review of *Blind Ambition: The White House Years*, by

John Dean, and *Chief Counsel: Inside the Ervin Committee*, by Samuel
    Dash, in the *New York Times Book Review*, October 31, 1976, pp. 1, 12.
Lukas, J. Anthony. Review of *"I Gave Them a Sword": Behind the Scenes
    of the Nixon Interviews*, by David Frost, in the *New York Times Book
    Review*, February 26, 1978, pp. 9, 31.
MacKenzie, John P. "Court Hears Watergate Tapes Case," *Washington Post*,
    p. A1, A17.
McGeever, Patrick J. "Guilty, Yes; Impeachment, No": Some Empirical Find-
    ings," *Political Science Quarterly*, Vol. 89, June 1974, pp. 289–299.
Magnuson, Edward. "Post-Mortem: The Unmaking of a President," *Time*,
    May 12, 1975, pp. 72–76.
Mailer, Norman. "A Harlot High and Low: Reconnoitering Through the Secret
    Government," *New York*, August 16, 1976, pp. 22–46.
"Man Proposes but the Court Disposes," *National Review*, August 16, 1974,
    pp. 904–907.
Mason, A. T. "Burger Court in Historical Persective," *Political Science Quart-
    erly*, March 1974, pp. 27–45.
Mazlish, Bruce. "Mr. Nixon's 'Performance'," *Washington Post*, November
    26, 1973, p. A20.
Mee, C. L. "Terminal Madness," *Horizon*, Autumn 1976, pp. 104–105.
Methen, E. H. "Chief Justice Burger Balances the Scales," *Reader's Digest*,
    April 1975, pp. 121–125.
Miller, William Lee. "An American Failure Story," *Commonweal*, September
    6, 1974, pp. 476–478.
Miller, William Lee. "Some Notes on Watergate and America," *Yale Review*,
    Vol. 63 (March 1974), pp. 321–332.
"Mission Impossible: The Watergate Bunglers," *Harper's*, October 1974, pp.
    51–58.
Mitgang, Herbert. "How a Psychiatrist 'Analyzed' Nixon," *New York Times*,
    April 7, 1977, p. 23.
Morgenthau, Hans. "The Aborted Nixon Revolution," *New Republic*, August
    11, 1973, pp. 17–19.
Muller, Rene J. "The Fictional Richard Nixon," *Nation*, July 6, 1974, pp.
    6–11.
Nathan, James. "Did Kissinger Leak the Big One?" *Washington Monthly*,
    September 1974, pp. 25–27.
Neustadt, Richard. "The Constraining of the President," *New York Times
    Magazine*, October 14, 1973, pp. 38–39, 110–117.
Nobile, Philip. "Psychohistory: A Controversial Discipline," *New York Times*,
    October 10, 1976, IV, p. 7.
Nolan, Martin. "The Man Who Could Push Richard Nixon Over the Edge,"
    New York, December 24, 1973, pp. 38–42.
Norton, Thomas J. "The Supreme Court's Five to Four Decisions," *American
    Bar Association Journal*, Vol. 9 (July 1923), pp. 417–420.
Osborne, John. "Nixon Postscript: The Unmasking of a President," *New
    Republic*, September 7, 1974, pp. 10–13.

Osborne, John. "Was Nixon 'Sick of Mind'?" *New York*, April 21, 1975, pp. 37–45.

Prescott, Peter S. "Presidential Deceit," review of *The Time of Illusion*, by Jonathan Schell, in *Newsweek*, January 12, 1976, p. 65.

Reeves, Richard. Review of the *The Final Days*, by Bob Woodward and Carl Bernstein, in the *New York Times Book Review*, April 18, 1976, pp. 1–2.

Reeves, Richard. "Memo to a Congressman: The Argument for Impeachment," *New York*, February 11, 1974, pp. 6–7.

Reeves, Richard. "Nixon in the Twilight Zone," *New York*, November 5, 1973, pp. 44–45.

Reichley, A. James. "Getting at the Roots of Watergate," *Fortune*, July 1973, pp. 91–93.

"Richard Nixon Stumbles at the Brink," *Time*, October 29, 1973, pp. 12–19.

Richardson, Elliot. "The Saturday Night Massacre," *Atlantic*, March 1976, pp. 40–44 + .

Rogow, Arnold. Review of *In Search of Nixon: A Psychohistorical Inquiry*, by Bruce Mazlish, in *Political Science Quarterly*, Vol. 87 (December 1972), pp. 675–676.

Safire, William. "Last Days in the Bunker," *New York Times Magazine*, August 18, 1974, p. 6.

Shannon, William V. Review of *Stonewall: The Real Story of the Watergate Prosecution*, by Richard Ben-Veniste and George Frampton, Jr., in the *New York Times Book Review*, May 8, 1977, pp. 7, 39.

Shawcross, William. Review of *Breach of Faith: The Fall of Richard Nixon*, by Theodore H. White, in the *New York Review of Books*, July 17, 1975, pp. 6, 10–11.

Sherrill, Robert. Review of *The Time of Illusion*, by Jonathan Schell, in the *New York Times Book Review*, January 18, 1976, pp. 1–2.

St. George, Andrew. "The Cold War Comes Home," *Harper's*, November 1973, pp. 68–82.

Stephenson, D. Grier. "The Mild Magistracy of the Law," *Intellect* (February 1975), pp. 288–292.

Stokes, Geoffrey. "The Story of P," *Harper's*, October 1974, pp. 6–12.

Totenberg, Nina. "Behind the Marble, Beneath the Robes," *New York Times Magazine*, March 16, 1975, p. 15.

Ungar, Sanford J. "The Undoing of the Justice Department," *Atlantic*, January 1974, pp. 29–34.

"The United States v. Richard M. Nixon, President et al.," *Time*, July 22, 1974, pp. 10–12.

"A Very Definitive Decision," *Newsweek*, August 5, 1974, pp. 24–36.

Waskow, Arthur L. "Impeachment Is Only a Crossroads," *Nation*, February 9, 1974, pp. 174–179.

Ways, Max. "Watergate as a Case Study in Management," *Fortune*, November 1973, pp. 109–111.

Wechsler, James. "The Fantasy World of 'Psychohistory'," *New York Post*, October 21, 1977, p. 31.

White, William S. "The Mood Changes on Capitol Hill," *Washington Post*, September 8, 1973, p. A15.

Wiener, Jon. "Tocqueville, Marx, Weber, Nixon: Watergate in Theory," *Dissent*, Spring 1976, pp. 171–180.

Wills, Garry. "Heroic Darkness," review of *The Ends of Power*, by H. R. Haldeman, and *With Nixon*, by Raymond Price, *New York Review of Books*, April 6, 1978, pp. 3–4.

Wills, Garry. "The Tyranny of Weakness," *Playboy*, December 1973, pp. 117 + .

Wrong, Dennis. "Watergate: Symptom of What Sickness?" *Dissent*, Fall 1974, pp. 501–507.

In addition to the cited pieces, the following sources have been extensively reviewed:

New York Times
Washington Post
New Republic
Newsweek
Time
U.S. News and World Report

C. *Methodological Sources and Game Theory Applications*

Brams, Steven J. *Biblical Games: A Strategic Analysis of Stories in the Old Testament*. Cambridge: MIT Press, 1980.

Brams, Steven J., "Deception in 2 × 2 Games," *Journal of Peace Research*, Spring 1977, pp. 171–203.

Brams, Steven J. *Game Theory and Politics*. New York: Free Press, 1975.

Brams, Steven J. "Nonmyopic Equilibria in Games and Politics: Foundations for a Dynamic Theory of Strategy," New York University, unpublished paper 1980.

Brams, Steven J. *Paradoxes in Politics: An Introduction to the Nonobvious in Political Science*. New York: Free Press, 1976.

Brams, Steven J., and Muzzio, Douglas. "Game Theory and the White House Tapes Case," *Trial*, May 1977, pp. 48–53.

Brams, Steven J., and Muzzio, Douglas. "Unanimity in the Supreme Court: A Game-Theoretic Explanation of the Decision in the White House Tapes Case," *Public Choice*, Vol. 32 (Winter 1977), pp. 67–83.

Brams, Steven J., and Zagare, Frank. "Deception in Simple Voting Games," *Social Science Research*, September 1977, pp. 257–272.

Davis, Morton. *Game Theory: A Nontechnical Introduction*. New York: Basic Books, 1973.

Deutsch, Karl. *The Nerves of Government: Models of Political Communication and Control*. New York: Free Press, 1966.

Deutsch, Karl, and Riesebach, Leroy N. "Empirical Theory," in Haas Michael, and Kariel, Henry S., eds. *Approaches to the Study of Political Science*. Scranton, Pa.: Chandler Publishing Co., 1970.

Harsanyi, John C. "Rational-Choice Models of Political Behavior vs. Functionalist and Conformist Theories," *World Politics*, Vol. 21 (July 1969), pp. 513–538.

Howard, Nigel. "Examples of a Dynamic Theory of Games," *Peace Society (International) Papers*, Vol. 24, pp. 1–28.

Howard, Nigel. "The Game-Theoretic Breakdown of Rationality: Some Implications for Policy Analysis, University of Ottawa, 1976, unpublished paper.

Howard, Nigel. *Paradoxes of Rationality: Theory of Metagames and Rational Behavior*. Cambridge: Mit Press, 1971.

Kaplan, Abraham. *The Conduct of Inquiry: Methodology for Behavioral Science*. San Francisco: Chandler Publishing Co., 1964.

Luce, Duncan, and Raiffa, Howard. *Games and Decisions*. New York: John Wiley and Sons, Inc., 1957.

McDonald, John. *The Game of Business*. New York: Doubleday and Co., 1975.

Rapoport, Anatol. *Game Theory as a Theory of Conflict Resolution*. Boston: D. Reidel Publishing Co., 1974.

Rapoport, Anatol. *N-Person Game Theory: Concepts and Applications*. Ann Arbor: University of Michigan Press, 1970.

Rapoport, Anatol. *Two-Person Game Theory: The Essential Ideas*. Ann Arbor: University of Michigan Press, 1970.

Rapoport, Anatol, and Chammah, Albert. *Prisoner's Dilemma*. Ann Arbor: University of Michigan Press, 1970.

Rapoport, Anatol, and Guyer, Melvin. "A Taxonomy of 2×2 Games," *General Systems Yearbook*, Vol. 12 (1966), pp. 203–214.

Shubik, Martin. "The Uses of Game Theory," in Charlesworth, James C., ed. *Contemporary Political Analysis*. New York: Free Press, 1967.

Tullock, Gordon. "The Prisoner's Dilemma and Mutual Trust," *Ethics*, Vol. 77 (April 1967), pp. 229–230.

von Neumann, John, and Morgenstern, Oskar. *Theory of Games and Economic Behavior*, 2nd ed. Princeton: Princeton University Press, 1947.

Zagare, Frank. "Deception in Three-Person Games: An Analysis of Strategic Misrepresentation in Vietnam." Ph.D. dissertation, New York University, 1977.

Zagare, Frank. "A Game-Theoretic Analysis of the Vietnam Negotiations: Preferences and Strategies 1968–1973," *Journal of Conflict Resolution*, Vol. 21 (December 1977), pp. 663–684.

Zagare, Frank. "The Geneva Conference of 1954: A Case of Tacit Deception," *International Studies Quarterly*, Vol. 23 (September 1979), pp. 390–411.

Index